Letters from America

Letters from America

RUPERT BROOKE

Preface by HENRY JAMES

SIDGWICK & JACKSON
LONDON

First published in 1931 by
Sidgwick and Jackson Limited
Second impression 1947
Reprinted 1971
Reprinted 1987
First Paperback Edition 1989

ISBN 0-283-99849-0

Printed in Hong Kong
for Sidgwick and Jackson Limited
1 Tavistock Chambers, Bloomsbury Way
London WC1A 2SG

Note

THE author started in May 1913 on a journey to the United States, Canada, and the South Seas, from which he returned next year at the beginning of June. The first thirteen chapters of this book were written as letters to the *Westminster Gazette*. He would probably not have republished them in their present form, as he intended to write a longer book on his travels; but they are now printed with only the correction of a few evident slips.

The two remaining chapters appeared in the *New Statesman*, soon after the outbreak of war.

Thanks are due to the Editors who have allowed the republication of the articles.

E. M.

Contents

RUPERT BROOKE

NOTHING more generally or more recurrently solicits us, in the light of literature, I think, than the interest of our learning how the poet, the true poet, and above all the particular one with whom we may for the moment be concerned, has come into his estate, asserted and preserved his identity, worked out his question of sticking to that and to nothing else ; and has so been able to reach us and touch us *as* a poet, in spite of the accidents and dangers that must have beset this course. The chances and changes, the personal history of any absolute genius, draw us to watch his adventure with curiosity and inquiry, lead us on to win more of his secret and borrow more of his experience (I mean, needless to say, when we are at all critically minded) ; but there is something in the clear safe arrival of the poetic nature, in a given case, at the point of its free and happy exercise, that provokes, if not the cold impulse to challenge or cross-question it, at least the need of understanding so far as possible how, in a world in which difficulty and disaster are frequent, the most wavering and flickering of all fine flames has escaped extinction. We go back, we help ourselves to hang about the attestation of the first spark of the flame, and like to indulge in a fond notation of such facts as that of the air in which it was kindled and insisted on proceeding, or yet perhaps failed to proceed, to a larger combustion, and the draughts, blowing about the world, that were either, as may have happened, to quicken its native force or perhaps to extinguish it in a gust of undue violence. It is naturally when the poet has emerged unmistakeably clear, or has at a happy moment of his story seemed likely to, that our attention and our suspense in the matter are most intimately engaged ; and we are at any rate in general beset by the impression and haunted by the observed law, that the growth and the triumph of the faculty at its finest have been positively in proportion to certain rigours of circumstance.

It is doubtless not indeed so much that this appearance has been inveterate as that the quality of genius in fact associated with it is apt to strike us as the clearest we know. We think of Dante in harassed exile, of Shakespeare under sordidly professional stress, of Milton in exasperated exposure and material darkness ; we think of Burns and Chatterton, and Keats and Shelley and Coleridge, we think of Leopardi and Musset and Emily Brontë and Walt Whitman, as it is open to us surely to think even of Wordsworth, so harshly conditioned by his spareness and bareness and bleakness—all this in reference to the voices that have most proved their command of the ear of time, and with the various examples added of those claiming, or at best enjoying, but the slighter attention ; and their office thus mainly affects us as that of showing in how jostled, how frequently arrested and all but

defeated a hand, the torch could still be carried.
It is not of course for the countrymen of Byron
and of Tennyson and Swinburne, any more than
for those of Victor Hugo, to say nothing of those
of Edmond Rostand, to forget the occurrence on
occasion of high instances in which the dangers all
seem denied and only favour and facility recorded ;
but it would take more of these than we can begin
to set in a row to purge us of that prime determinant,
after all, of our affection for the great poetic muse,
the vision of the rarest sensibility and the largest
generosity we know kept by her at their pitch, kept
fighting for their life and insisting on their range
of expression, amid doubts and derisions and buffets,
even sometimes amid stones of stumbling quite
self-invited, that might at any moment have made
the loss of the precious clue really irremediable.
Which moral, so pointed, accounts assuredly for
half our interest in the poetic character—a sentiment
more unlikely than not, I think, to survive a sus-
tained succession of Victor Hugos and Rostands,
or of Byrons, Tennysons and Swinburnes. We
quite consciously miss in these bards, as we find
ourselves rather wondering even at our failure to
miss it in Shelley, that such " complications " as
they may have had to reckon with were not in
general of the cruelly troublous order, and that no
stretch of the view either of our own " theory of
art " or of our vivacity of passion as making trouble,
contributes perceptibly the required savour of the
pathetic. We cling, critically or at least experienti-
ally speaking, to our superstition, if not absolutely

to our approved measure, of this grace and proof;
and that truly, to cut my argument short, is what
sets us straight down before a sudden case in which
the old discrimination quite drops to the ground—
in which we neither on the one hand miss anything
that the general association could have given it,
nor on the other recognise the pomp that attends
the grand exceptions I have mentioned.

Rupert Brooke, young, happy, radiant, extraordinarily endowed and irresistibly attaching, vir-
tually met a soldier's death, met it in the stress of
action and the all but immediate presence of the
enemy; but he is before us as a new, a confounding
and superseding example altogether, an unprecedented image, formed to resist erosion by time or
vulgarisation by reference, of quickened possibilities,
finer ones than ever before, in the stuff poets may
be noted as made of. With twenty reasons fixing
the interest and the charm that will henceforth
abide in his name and constitute, as we may say,
his legend, he submits all helplessly to one in particular which is, for appreciation, the least personal
to him or inseparable from him, and he does this
because, while he is still in the highest degree of
the distinguished faculty and quality, we happen
to feel him even more markedly and significantly
"modern." This is why I speak of the mixture
of his elements as new, feeling that it governs his
example, put by it in a light which nothing else
could have equally contributed—so that Byron for
instance, who startled his contemporaries by taking
for granted scarce one of the articles that formed

their comfortable faith and by revelling in almost everything that made them idiots if he himself was to figure as a child of truth, looks to us, by any such measure, comparatively plated over with the impenetrable rococo of his own day. I speak, I hasten to add, not of Byron's volume, his flood and his fortune, but of his really having quarrelled with the temper and the accent of his age still more where they might have helped him to expression than where he but flew in their face. He hugged his pomp, whereas our unspeakably fortunate young poet of to-day, linked like him also, for consecration of the final romance, with the isles of Greece, took for *his* own the whole of the poetic consciousness he was born to, and moved about in it as a stripped young swimmer might have kept splashing through blue water and coming up at any point that friendliness and fancy, with every prejudice shed, might determine. Rupert expressed us *all*, at the highest tide of our actuality, and was the creature of a freedom restricted only by that condition of his blinding youth, which we accept on the whole with gratitude and relief—given that I qualify the condition as dazzling even to himself. How can it therefore not be interesting to see a little what the wondrous modern in him consisted of ?

I

What it first and foremost really comes to, I think, is the fact that at an hour when the civilised peoples are on exhibition, quite finally and sharply on show,

to each other and to the world, as they absolutely
never in all their long history have been before,
the English tradition (both of amenity and of energy,
I naturally mean), should have flowered at once into
a specimen so beautifully producible. Thousands
of other sentiments are of course all the while, in
different connections, at hand for us ; but it is of
the exquisite civility, the social instincts of the race,
poetically expressed, that I speak ; and it would
be hard to overstate the felicity of his fellow-country-
men's being able just now to say : " Yes, this,
with the imperfection of so many of our arrange-
ments, with the persistence of so many of our mis-
takes, with the waste of so much of our effort and
the weight of the many-coloured mantle of time
that drags so redundantly about us, this natural
accommodation of the English spirit, this frequent
extraordinary beauty of the English aspect, this
finest saturation of the English intelligence by its
most immediate associations, tasting as they mainly
do of the long past, this ideal image of English youth,
in a word, at once radiant and reflective, are things
that appeal to us as delightfully exhibitional beyond
a doubt, yet as drawn, to the last fibre, from the
very wealth of our own conscience and the very
force of our own history. We haven't, for such
an instance of our genius, to reach out to strange
places or across other, and otherwise productive,
tracts ; the exemplary instance himself has well-
nigh as a matter of course reached and revelled,
for that is exactly our way in proportion as we feel
ourselves clear. But the kind of experience so

entailed, of contribution so gathered, is just what
we wear easiest when we have been least stinted
of it, and what our English use of makes perhaps
our vividest reference to our thick-growing native
determinants."

Rupert Brooke, at any rate, the charmed com-
mentator may well keep before him, simply did all
the usual English things—under the happy provision
of course that he found them in his way at their best ;
and it was exactly most delightful in him that no
inordinate expenditure, no anxious extension of
the common plan, as " liberally " applied all about
him, had been incurred or contrived to predetermine
his distinction. It is difficult to express on the
contrary how peculiar a value attached to his having
simply " come in " for the general luck awaiting
any English youth who may not be markedly inapt
for the traditional chances. He could in fact easily
strike those who most appreciated him as giving
such an account of the usual English things—to
repeat the form of my allusion to them—as seemed
to address you to them, in their very considerable
number indeed, for any information about him that
might matter, but which left you wholly to judge
whether they seemed justified by their fruits. This
manner about them, as one may call it in general,
often contributes to your impression that they make
for a certain strain of related modesty which may
on occasion be one of their happiest effects ; it at
any rate, in days when my acquaintance with them
was slighter, used to leave me gaping at the treasure
of operation, the far recessional perspectives, it

took for granted and any offered demonstration of
the extent or the mysteries of which seemed unthink-
able just in proportion as the human resultant
testified in some one or other of his odd ways to their
influence.   He might not always be, at any rate on
first acquaintance, a resultant explosively human,
but there was in any case one reflection he could
always cause you to make : " What a wondrous
system it indeed must be which insists on flourishing
to all appearance under such an absence of advertised
or even of confessed relation to it as would do
honour to a vacuum produced by an air-pump ! "
The formulation, the approximate expression of
what the system at large might or mightn't do for
those in contact with it, became thus one's own
fitful care, with one's attention for a considerable
period doubtless dormant enough, but with the
questions always liable to revive before the individual case.

Rupert Brooke made them revive as soon as one
began to know him, or in other words made one want
to read back into him each of his promoting causes
without exception, to trace to some source in the
ambient air almost any one, at a venture, of his
aspects ; so precious a loose and careless bundle of
happy references did that inveterate trick of giving
the go-by to over-emphasis which he shared with
his general kind fail to prevent your feeling sure of
his having about him.   I think the liveliest interest
of these was that while not one of them was signally
romantic, by the common measure of the great
English amenity, they yet hung together, rein-

forcing and enhancing each other, in a way that
seemed to join their hands for an incomparably
educative or civilising process, the great mark of
which was that it took some want of amenability
in particular subjects to betray anything like a gap.
I do not mean of course to say that gaps, and occasionally of the most flagrant, were made so supremely
difficult of occurrence ; but only that the effect,
in the human resultants who kept these, and with
the least effort, most in abeyance, was a thing one
wouldn't have had different by a single shade. I
am not sure that such a case of the recognisable
was the better established by the fact of Rupert's
being one of the three sons of a house-master at
Rugby, where he was born in 1887 and where he
lost his father in 1910, the elder of his brothers
having then already died and the younger being
destined to fall in battle at the allied Front, shortly
after he himself had succumbed ; but the circumstance I speak of gives a peculiar and an especially
welcome consecration to that perceptible play in
him of the inbred " public school " character the
bloom of which his short life had too little time to
remove and which one wouldn't for the world not
have been disposed to note, with everything else,
in the beautiful complexity of his attributes. The
fact was that if one liked him—and I may as well
say at once that few young men, in our time, can
have gone through life under a greater burden,
more easily carried and kept in its place, of being
liked—one liked absolutely everything about him,
without the smallest exception ; so that he appeared

to convert before one's eyes all that happened to
him, or that had or that ever might, not only to his
advantage as a source of life and experience, but to
the enjoyment on its own side of a sort of illustrational
virtue or glory This appearance of universal
assimilation—often indeed by incalculable ironic
reactions which were of the very essence of the restless
young intelligence rejoicing in its gaiety—made
each part of his rich consciousness, so rapidly ac-
quired, cling, as it were, to the company of all the
other parts, so as at once neither to miss any touch
of the luck (one keeps coming back to that), incurred
by them, or to let them suffer any want of its own
rightness. It was as right, through the spell he
cast altogether, that he should have come into the
world and have passed his boyhood in that Rugby
home, as that he should have been able later on to
wander as irrepressibly as the spirit moved him,
or as that he should have found himself fitting as
intimately as he was very soon to do into any number
of the incalculabilities, the intellectual at least, of
the poetic temperament. He had them all, he gave
himself in his short career up to them all—and I
confess that, partly for reasons to be further developed, I am unable even to guess what they might
eventually have made of him ; which is of course
what brings us round again to that view of him as
the young poet with absolutely nothing but his
generic spontaneity to trouble about, the young
poet profiting for happiness by a general condition
unprecedented for young poets, that I began by
indulging in.

He went from Rugby to Cambridge, where, after a while, he carried off a Fellowship at King's, and where, during a short visit there in " May week," or otherwise early in June 1909, I first, and as I was to find, very unforgettingly, met him. He reappears to me as with his felicities all most promptly divinable, in that splendid setting of the river at the " backs " ; as to which indeed I remember vaguely wondering what it was left to such a place to do with the added, the verily wasted, grace of such a person, or how even such a person could hold his own, as who should say, at such a pitch of simple scenic perfection. Any difficulty dropped, however, to the reconciling vision ; for that the young man was publicly and responsibly a poet seemed the fact a little over-officiously involved—to the promotion of a certain surprise (on one's own part) at his having to " be " anything. It was to come over me still more after-wards that nothing of that or of any other sort need really have rested on him with a weight of obligation, and in fact I cannot but think that life might have been seen and felt to suggest to him, in an exposed unanimous conspiracy, that his status should be left to the general sense of others, ever so many others, who would sufficiently take care of it, and that such a fine rare case was accordingly as arguable as it possibly *could* be—with the pure, undischarged poetry of him and the latent presumption of his dying for his country the only things to gainsay it. The question was to a certain extent crude, " Why *need* he be a poet, why need he so specialise ? " but if this was so it was only, it was already, symp-

tomatic óf the interesting final truth that he was
to testify to his function in the unparalleled way.
He was going to have the life (the unanimous conspiracy so far achieved *that*), was going to have it
under no more formal guarantee than that of his
appetite and genius for it ; and this was to help us
all to the complete appreciation of him.   No single
scrap of the English fortune at its easiest and truest
—which means of course with every vulgarity dropped
out—but was to brush him as by the readiest in-
stinctive wing, never over-straining a point or achiev-
ing a miracle to do so ;   only trusting his exquisite
imagination and temper to respond to the succession
of his opportunities.   It is in the light of what this
succession could in the most natural and most familiar
way in the world amount to for him that we find
this idea of a beautiful crowning modernness above
all to meet his case.   The promptitude, the perception, the understanding, the quality of humour
and sociability, the happy lapses in the logic of
inward reactions (save for their all infallibly being
poetic), of which he availed himself consented to be
as illustrational as any fondest friend could wish,
whether the subject of the exhibition was aware of
the degree or not, and made his vivacity of vision,
his exercise of fancy and irony, of observation at
its freest, inevitable—while at the same time setting
in motion no machinery of experience in which his
curiosity, or in other words, the quickness of his
familiarity, didn't move faster than anything else.

II

I owe to his intimate and devoted friend Mr Edward Marsh the communication of many of his letters, these already gathered into an admirable brief memoir which is yet to appear and which will give ample help in the illustrative way to the pages to which the present remarks form a preface, and which are collected from the columns of the London evening journal in which they originally saw the light. The " literary baggage " of his short course consists thus of his two slender volumes of verse and of these two scarcely stouter sheafs of correspondence [1]—though I should add that the hitherto unpublished letters enjoy the advantage of a commemorative and interpretative commentary, at the Editor's hands, which will have rendered the highest service to each matter. That even these four scant volumes tell the whole story, or fix the whole image, of the fine young spirit they are concerned with we certainly hold back from allowing ; his case being in an extraordinary degree that of a creature on whom the gods had smiled their brightest, and half of whose manifestation therefore was by the simple act of presence and of direct communication. He did in fact specialise, to repeat my term ; only since, as one reads him, whether in verse or in prose, that distinguished readability seems all the specialisation one need invoke, so when the question was of the gift that made of his face to face address a circum-

[1] There remain also to be published a book on John Webster, and a prose play in one act.—E.M.

stance so complete in itself as apparently to cover all
the ground, leaving no margin either, an activity
to the last degree justified appeared the only name
for one's impression. The moral of all which is
doubtless that these brief, if at the same time very
numerous, moments of his quick career formed
altogether as happy a time, in as happy a place, to
be born to as the student of the human drama has
ever caught sight of—granting always, that is, that
some actor of the scene has been thoroughly up to
his part. Such was the sort of recognition, assuredly,
under which Rupert played *his*—that of his lending
himself to every current and contact, the " newer,"
the later fruit of time, the better ; only this not
because any particular one was an agitating revelation, but because with due sensibility, with a
restless inward ferment, at the centre of them all,
what could he possibly so much feel like as the heir
of all the ages ?   I remember his originally giving
me, though with no shade of imputable intention,
the sense of his just *being* that, with the highest
amiability—the note in him that, as I have hinted,
one kept coming back to ; so that during a long wait
for another glimpse of him I thought of the practice and function so displayed as wholly engaging,
took for granted his keeping them up with equal
facility and pleasure.   Nothing could have been more
delightful accordingly, later on, in renewal of the
personal acquaintance than to gather that this was
exactly what had been taking place, and with an
inveteracy as to which his letters are a full docu-
mentation.   Whatever his own terms for the process

might be had he been brought to book, and though
the variety of his terms for anything and everything
was the very play, and even the measure, of his
talent, the most charmed and conclusive description
of him was that no young man had ever so naturally
taken on under the pressure of life the poetic nature,
and shaken it so free of every encumbrance by simply
wearing it as he wore his complexion or his outline.

That, then, was the way the imagination followed
him with its luxury of confidence : he was doing
everything that could be done in the time (since
this was the modernest note), but performing each
and every finest shade of these blest acts with a
poetic punctuality that was only matched by a
corresponding social sincerity. I recall perfectly
my being sure of it all the while, even if with little
current confirmation beyond that supplied by his
first volume of verse ; and the effect of the whole
record is now to show that such a conclusion was
quite extravagantly right. He *was* constantly doing
all the things, and this with a reckless freedom, as
it might be called, that really dissociated the responsibility of the precious character from anything like
conscious domestic coddlement to a point at which
no troubled young singer, none, that is, equally
troubled, had perhaps ever felt he could afford to
dissociate it. Rupert's resources for affording, in
the whole connection, were his humour, his irony,
his need, under every quiver of inspiration, toward
whatever end, to be amused and amusing, and to
find above all that this could never so much occur
as by the application of his talent, of which he was

perfectly conscious, to his own case. He carried
his case with him, for purposes of derision as much
as for any others, wherever he went, and how he
went everywhere, thus blissfully burdened, is what
meets us at every turn on his printed page. My
only doubt about him springs in fact from the
question of whether he knew that the earthly felicity
enjoyed by him, his possession of the exquisite
temperament linked so easily to the irrepressible
experience, was a thing to make of the young Briton
of the then hour so nearly the spoiled child of history
that one wanted something in the way of an extra
guarantee to feel soundly sure of him. I come back
once more to his having apparently never dreamt
of any stretch of the point of liberal allowance, of
so-called adventure, on behalf of " development,"
never dreamt of any stretch but that of the imagination itself indeed—quite a different matter and even
if it too were at moments to recoil ; it was so true
that the general measure of his world as to what it
might be prompt and pleasant and in the day's
work or the day's play to " go in for " was exactly
the range that tinged all his education as liberal, the
education the free design of which he had left so
short a way behind him when he died.

Just there was the luck attendant of the coincidence
of his course with the moment at which the proceeding hither and yon to the tune of almost any
" happy thought," and in the interest of almost
any branch of culture or invocation of response that
might be more easily improvised than not, could
positively strike the observer as excessive, as in

fact absurd, for the formation of taste or the enrich-
ment of genius, unless the principle of these values
had in a particular connection been subjected in
advance to some challenge or some test. Why
should it take such a flood of suggestion, such a
luxury of acquaintance and contact, only to make
superficial specimens ? Why shouldn't the art of
living inward a little more, and thereby of digging
a little deeper or pressing a little further, rather
modestly replace the enviable, always the enviable,
young Briton's enormous range of alternatives in
the way of question-begging movement, the way
of vision and of non-vision, the enormous habit
of holidays ? If one could have made out once for
all that holidays were proportionately and infallibly
inspiring one would have ceased thoughtfully to
worry ; but the question was as it stood an old
story, even though it might freshly radiate, on
occasion, under the recognition that the seed-
smothered patch of soil flowered, when it did flower,
with a fragrance all its own. This concomitant,
however, always dangled, that if it were put to us,
" Do you really mean you would rather they should
not perpetually have been again for a look-in at
Berlin, or an awfully good time at Munich, or a
rush round Sicily, or a dash through the States to
Japan, with whatever like rattling renewals ? "
you would after all shrink from the responsibility
of such a restriction before being clear as to what
you would suggest in its place. Rupert went on
reading-parties from King's to Lulworth for instance,
which the association of the two places, the two

so extraordinarily finished scenes, causes to figure
as a sort of preliminary flourish ; and everything
that came his way after that affects me as the blest
indulgence in flourish upon flourish. This was not
in the least the air, or the desire, or the pretension
of it, but the unfailing felicity just kept catching
him up, just left him never wanting nor waiting
for some pretext to roam, or indeed only the more
responsively to stay, doing either, whichever it might
be, as a form of highly intellectualised " fun." He
didn't overflow with shillings, yet so far as roving
was concerned the practice was always easy, and
perhaps the adorably whimsical lyric, contained
in his second volume of verse, on the pull of Grantchester at his heartstrings, as the old vicarage of that
sweet adjunct to Cambridge could present itself to
him in a Berlin café, may best exemplify the sort of
thing that was represented, in one way and another,
by his taking his most ultimately English ease.

Whatever Berlin or Munich, to speak of them only,
could do or fail to do for him, how can one not rejoice
without reserve in the way he felt what he did feel
as poetic reaction of the liveliest and finest, with
the added interest of its often turning at one and the
same time to the fullest sincerity and to a perversity
of the most " evolved " ?—since I can not dispense
with that sign of truth. Never was a young singer
either less obviously sentimentál or less addicted
to the mere twang of the guitar ; at the same time
that it was always his personal experience or his
curious, his not a little defiantly excogitated, inner
vision that he sought to catch ; some of the odd

fashion of his play with which latter seems on occasion to preponderate over the truly pleasing poet's appeal to beauty or cultivated habit of grace. Odd enough, no doubt, that Rupert should appear to have had well-nigh in horror the cultivation of grace for its own sake, as we say, and yet should really not have disfigured his poetic countenance by a single touch quotable as showing this. The medal of the mere pleasant had always a reverse for him, and it was generally in that substitute he was most interested. We catch in him reaction upon reaction, the succession of these conducing to his entirely unashamed poetic complexity, and of course one observation always to be made about him, one reminder always to be gratefully welcomed, is that we are dealing after all with one of the *youngest* quantities of art and character taken together that ever arrived at an irresistible appeal. His irony, his liberty, his pleasantry, his paradox, and what I have called his perversity, are all nothing if not young ; and I may as well say at once for him that I find in the imagination of their turning in time, dreadful time, to something more balanced and harmonised, a difficulty insuperable. The self-consciousness, the poetic, of his so free figuration (in verse, only in verse, oddly enough) of the unpleasant to behold, to touch, or even to smell, was certainly, I think, nothing if not " self-conscious," but there were so many things in his consciousness, which was never in the least unpeopled, that it would have been a rare chance had his projection of the self that we are so apt to make an object of invidious

allusion stayed out. What it all really most comes
to, you feel again, is that none of his impulses pros-
pered in solitude, or, for that matter, were so much as
permitted to mumble their least scrap there; he was
predestined and condemned to sociability, which
no league of neglect could have deprived him of
even had it speculatively tried : whereby what was
it but his own image that he most saw reflected in
other faces ? It would still have been there, it
couldn't possibly have succeeded in not being, even
had he closed his eyes to it with elaborate tightness.
The only neglect must have been on his own side,
where indeed it did take form in that of as signal
an opportunity to become " spoiled," probably,
as ever fell in a brilliant young man's way : so that
to help out my comprehension of the unsightly and
nsavoury, sufficiently wondered at, with which
his muse repeatedly embraced the occasion to associ-
ate herself, I take the thing for a declaration of
the idea that he might himself prevent the spoiling
so far as possible. He could in fact prevent nothing,
the wave of his fortune and his favour continuing
so to carry him ; which is doubtless one of the
reasons why, through our general sense that nothing
could possibly not be of the last degree of rightness
in him, what would have been wrong in others,
literally in any creature *but* him, like for example
" A Channel Passage " of his first volume, simply
puts on, while this particular muse stands anxiously
by, a kind of dignity of experiment quite consistent
with our congratulating her, at the same time, as
soon as it is over. What was " A Channel Passage "

thus but a flourish marked with the sign of all his flourishes, that of being a success and having fruition ? Though it performed the extraordinary feat of directing the contents of the poet's stomach straight at the object of his displeasure, we feel that, by some excellent grace, the object is not at all reached —too many things, and most of all, too innocently enormous a cynicism, standing in the way and themselves receiving the tribute ; having in a word, impatient young cynicism as they are, *that* experience as well as various things.

III

No detail of Mr Marsh's admirable memoir may I allow myself to anticipate. I can only announce it as a picture, with all the elements in iridescent fusion, of the felicity that fairly dogged Rupert's steps, as we may say, and that never allowed him to fall below its measure. We shall read into it even more relations than nominally appear, and every one of them again a flourish, every one of them a connection with his time, a " sampling " of it at its most multitudinous and most characteristic ; every one of them too a record of the state of some other charmed, not less than charming party—even when the letter-writer's expression of the interest, the amusement, the play of fancy, of taste, of whatever sort of appreciation or reaction for his own spirit, is the ostensible note. This is what I mean in especial by the constancy with which, and the cost at which, perhaps not less, for others, the poetic sensibility was maintained and guaranteed. It was as genuine as if he had been a bard perched on an eminence with a harp, and yet it was arranged for, as we may say, by the close consensus of those who had absolutely to know their relation with him but as a delight and who wanted therefore to keep him, to the last point, true to himself. His complete curiosity and sociability might have made him, on these lines, factitious, if it had not happened that the people he so variously knew and the contacts he enjoyed were just of the kind to promote most his facility and vivacity and intelligence of life. They were all young together, allowing for three or four notable, by which I mean far from the least responsive, exceptions ; they were all fresh and free and acute and aware and in " the world," when not out of it ; all together at the high speculative, the high talkative pitch of the initiational stage of these latest years, the informed and animated, the so consciously non-benighted, geniality of which was to make him the clearest and most projected poetic case, with the question of difficulty and doubt and frustration most solved, the question of the immediate and its implications most in order for him, that it was possible to conceive. He had found at once to his purpose a wondrous enough old England, an England breaking out into numberless assertions of a new awareness, into liberties of high and clean, even when most sceptical and discursive, young intercourse ; a carnival of half anxious and half elated criticism, all framed and backgrounded in

still richer accumulations, both moral and material,
or, as who should say, pictorial, of the matter of
course and the taken for granted. Nothing could
have been in greater contrast, one cannot too much
insist, to the situation of the traditional lonely
lyrist who yearns for connections and relations yet
to be made and whose difficulty, lyrical, emotional,
personal, social or intellectual, has thereby so little
in common with any embarrassment of choice.
The author of the pages before us was perhaps
the young lyrist, in all the annals of verse,
who, having the largest luxury of choice, yet
remained least " demoralised " by it—how little
demoralised he was to round off his short history
by showing.

It was into these conditions, thickening and
thickening, in their comparative serenity, up to
the eleventh hour, that the War came smashing
down ; but of the basis, the great garden ground,
all green and russet and silver, all a tissue of distinguished and yet so easy occasions, so improvised
extensions, which they had already placed at his
service and that of his extraordinarily amiable and
constantly enlarged " set " for the exercise of *their*
dealing with the rest of the happy earth in punctuat-
ing interludes, it is the office of our few but precious
documents to enable us to judge. The interlude
that here concerns us most is that of the year spent
in his journey round a considerable part of the
world in 1913-14, testifying with a charm that
increases as he goes to that quest of unprejudiced
culture, the true poetic, the vision of the life of

man, which was to prove the liveliest of his impulses. It was not indeed under the flag of that research that he offered himself for the Army almost immediately after his return to England—and even if when a young man was so essentially a poet we need see no act in him as a prosaic alternative. The misfortune of this set of letters from New York and Boston, from Canada and Samoa, addressed, for the most part, to a friendly London evening journal is, alas, in the fact that they are of so moderate a quantity; for we make him out as steadily more vivid and delightful while his opportunity grows. He is touching at first, inevitably quite juvenile, in the measure of his good faith; we feel him not a little lost and lonely and stranded in the New York pandemonium—obliged to throw himself upon sky-scrapers and the overspread blackness pricked out in a flickering fury of imaged advertisement for want of some more interesting view of character and manners. We long to take him by the hand and show him finer lights—eyes of but meaner range, after all, being adequate to the gape at the vertical business blocks and the lurid sky-clamour for more dollars. We feel in a manner his sensibility wasted and would fain turn it on to the capture of deeper meanings. But we must leave him to himself and to youth's facility of wonder; he is amused, beguiled, struck on the whole with as many differences as we could expect, and sufficiently reminded, no doubt, of the number of words he is restricted to. It is moreover his sign, as it is that of the poetic turn of mind in general that we seem to catch him alike in antici-

pations or divinations, and in lapses and freshnesses,
of experience that surprise us. He makes various
reflections, some of them all perceptive and ingenious
—as about the faces, the men's in particular, seen
in the streets, the public conveyances and elsewhere ;
though falling a little short, in his friendly wondering
way, of that bewildered apprehension of monotony
of type, of modelling lost in the desert, which we
might have expected of him, and of the question
above all of what is destined to become of that
more and more vanishing quantity the American
nose other than Judaic.

What we note in particular is that he likes, to
all appearance, many more things than he doesn't,
and how superlatively he is struck with the promptitude and wholeness of the American welcome and
of all its friendly service. What it is but too easy,
with the pleasure of having known him, to read
into all this is the operation of his own irresistible
quality, and of the state of felicity he clearly created
just by appearing as a party to the social relation.
He moves and circulates to our vision as so naturally,
so beautifully undesigning a weaver of that spell,
that we feel comparatively little of the story told
even by his diverted report of it ; so much fuller
a report would surely proceed, could we appeal to
their memory, their sense of poetry, from those
into whose ken he floated. It is impossible not to
figure him, to the last felicity, as he comes and goes,
presenting himself always with a singular effect
both of suddenness and of the readiest rightness ;
we should always have liked to be there, wherever

it was, for the justification of our own fond confidence
and the pleasure of seeing it unfailingly spread and
spread. The ironies and paradoxes of his verse,
in all this record, fall away from him ; he takes to
direct observation and accepts with perfect good-
humour any hazards of contact, some of the shocks
of encounter proving more muffled for him than
might, as I say, have been feared—witness the
American Jew with whom he appears to have spent
some hours in Canada ; and of course the " word "
of the whole thing is that he simply reaped at every
turn the harmonising benefit that his presence
conferred. This it is in especial that makes us
regret so much the scanting, as we feel it, of his
story ; it deprives us in just that proportion of
certain of the notes of his appearance and his
" success." *There* was the poetic fact involved—
that, being so gratefully apprehended everywhere,
his own response was inevitably prescribed and
pitched as the perfect friendly and genial and liberal
thing. Moreover, the value of his having so let
himself loose in the immensity tells more at each
step in favour of his style ; the pages from Canada,
where as an impressionist, he increasingly finds his
feet, and even finds to the same increase a certain
comfort of association, are better than those from
the States, while those from the Pacific Islands
rapidly brighten and enlarge their inspiration. This
part of his adventure was clearly the great success
and fell in with his fancy, amusing and quickening
and rewarding him, more than anything in the whole
revelation. He lightly performs the miracle, to

my own sense, which R. L. Stevenson, which even Pierre Loti, taking however long a rope, had not performed ; he charmingly conjures away—though in this prose more than in the verse of his second volume—the marked tendency of the whole exquisite region to insist on the secret of its charm, when incorrigibly moved to do so, only at the expense of its falling a little flat, or turning a little stale, on our hands. I have for myself at least marked the tendency, and somehow felt it point a graceless moral, the moral that as there are certain faces too well produced by nature to be producible again by the painter, the portraitist, so there are certain combinations of earthly ease, of the natural and social art of giving pleasure, which fail of character, or accent, even of the power to interest, under the strain of transposition or of emphasis. Rupert, with an instinct of his own, transposes and insists only in the right degree ; or what it doubtless comes to is that we simply see him arrested by so vivid a picture of the youth of the world at its blandest as to make all his culture seem a waste and all his questions a vanity. That is apparently the very effect of the Pacific life as those who dip into it seek, or feel that they are expected to seek, to report it ; but it reports itself somehow through these pages, smilingly cools itself off in them, with the lightest play of the fan ever placed at its service. Never, clearly, had he been on such good terms with the hour, never found the life of the senses so anticipate the life of the imagination, or the life of the imagination so content itself with the life of the senses ; it is all an abundance of amphibious felicity—he was as incessant and insatiable a swimmer as if he had been a triton framed for a decoration ; and one half makes out that some low-lurking instinct, some vague foreboding of what awaited him, on his own side the globe, in the air of so-called civilisation, prompted him to drain to the last drop the whole perfect negation of the acrid. He might have been waiting for the tide of the insipid to begin to flow again, as it seems ever doomed to do when the acrid, the saving acrid, has already ebbed ; at any rate his holiday had by the end of the springtime of 1914 done for him all it could, without a grain of waste—his assimilations being neither loose nor literal, and he came back to England as promiscuously qualified, as variously quickened, as his best friends could wish for fine production and fine illustration in some order still awaiting sharp definition. Never certainly had the free poetic sense in him more rejoiced in an incorruptible sincerity.

IV

He was caught up of course after the shortest interval by the strong rush of that general inspiration in which at first all differences, all individual relations to the world he lived in, seemed almost ruefully or bewilderedly to lose themselves. The pressing thing was of a sudden that youth was youth and genius community and sympathy. He plunged into that full measure of these things which simply made and spread itself as it gathered them in, made itself of responses and faiths and understandings that were all the while in themselves acts of curiosity, romantic and poetic throbs and wonderments, with reality, as it seemed to call itself, breaking in after a fashion that left the whole past pale, and that yet could flush at every turn with meanings and visions borrowing their expression from whatever had, among those squandered preliminaries, those too merely sportive intellectual and critical values, happened to make most for the higher truth. Of the successions of his matter of history at this time Mr Marsh's memoir is the infinitely touching record —touching after the fact, but to the accompaniment even at the time of certain now almost ineffable reflections ; this especially, I mean, if one happened to be then not wholly without familiar vision of him. What could strike one more, for the immense occasion, than the measure that might be involved in it of desolating and heart-breaking waste, waste of quality, waste for that matter of quantity, waste of all the rich redundancies, all the light and all the golden store, which up to then had formed the very price and grace of life ? Yet out of the depths themselves of this question rose the other, the tormenting, the sickening and at the same time the strangely sustaining, of why, since the offering couldn't at best be anything but great, it wouldn't be great just in proportion to its purity, or in other words its wholeness, everything in it that could make it most radiant and restless. Exquisite at such times the hushed watch of the mere hovering spectator unrelieved by any action of his own to take, which consists at once of so much wonder for why the finest of the fine should, to the sacrifice of the faculty we most know them by, have to become mere morsels in the huge promiscuity, and of the thrill of seeing that they add more than ever to our knowledge and our passion, which somehow thus becomes at the same time an unfathomable abyss.

Rupert, who had joined the Naval Brigade, took part in the rather distractedly improvised—as it at least at the moment appeared—movement for the relief of the doomed Antwerp, but was, later on, after the return of the force so engaged, for a few days in London, whither he had come up from camp in Dorsetshire, briefly invalided ; thanks to which accident I had on a couple of occasions my last sight of him. It was all auspiciously, well-nigh extravagantly, congruous ; nothing certainly could have been called more modern than all the elements and suggestions of his situation for the hour, the very spot in London that could best serve as a centre for vibrations the keenest and most various ; a challenge to the appreciation of life, to that of the whole range of the possible English future, at its most uplifting. He had not yet so much struck me as an admirable nature *en disponibilité* and such as any cause, however high, might swallow up with a sense of being the sounder and sweeter for. More definitely perhaps the young poet, with all the wind alive in his sails, was as evident there in the guise of the young soldier and the thrice welcome young friend, who yet, I all recognisably remember, insisted on himself as little as ever in either character, and seemed even more disposed than usual not to let his intelligibility interfere with his modesty. He promptly recovered and returned to camp, whence it was testified that his specific practical aptitude, under the lively call, left nothing to be desired—a fact that expressed again, to the perception of his circle, with what truth the spring of inspiration worked in him, in the sense, I mean, that his imagination itself shouldered and made light of the material load. It had not yet, at the same time, been more associatedly active in a finer sense ; my own next apprehension of it at least was in reading the five admirable sonnets that had been published in " New Numbers " after the departure of his contingent for the campaign at the Dardanelles. To read these in the light of one's personal knowledge of him was to draw from them, inevitably, a meaning still deeper seated than their noble beauty, an authority, of the purest, attended with which his name inscribes itself in its own character on the great English scroll. The impression, the admiration, the anxiety settled immediately—to my own sense at least— as upon something that would but too sharply feed them, falling in as it did with that whole particularly animated vision of him of which I have spoken. He had never seemed more animated with our newest and least deluded, least conventionalised life and perception and sensibility, and that formula

of his so distinctively fortunate, his overflowing
share in our most developed social heritage which
had already glimmered, began with this occasion
to hang about him as one of the aspects, really a
shining one, of his fate.

So I remember irrepressibly thinking and feeling,
unspeakably apprehending, in a word ; and so the
whole exquisite exhalation of his own consciousness
in the splendid sonnets, attach whatever essentially
or exclusively poetic value to it we might, baffled
or defied us as with a sort of supreme rightness.
Everything about him of keenest and brightest
(yes, absolutely of brightest) suggestion made so
for his having been charged with every privilege,
every humour, of our merciless actuality, our fatal
excess of opportunity, that what indeed could the
full assurance of this be but that, finding in him
the most charming object in its course, the great
tide was to lift him and sweep him away ?   Questions
and reflections after the fact perhaps, yet haunting
for the time and during the short interval that was
still to elapse—when, with the sudden news that he
had met his doom, an irrepressible " of course, of
course ! " contributed its note well-nigh of support.
It was as if the peculiar richness of his youth had
itself marked its limit, so that what his own spirit
was inevitably to feel about his " chance "—inevitably because both the high pitch of the romantic
and the ironic and the opposed abyss of the real
came together in it—required, in the wondrous
way, the consecration of the event.   The event came
indeed not in the manner prefigured by him in the

repeatedly perfect line, that of the received death-
stroke, the fall in action, discounted as such ; which
might have seemed very much because even the
harsh logic and pressure of history were tender of
him at the last and declined to go through more
than the form of their function, discharging it with
the least violence and surrounding it as with a
legendary light. He was taken ill, as an effect of
blood-poisoning, on his way from Alexandria to
Gallipoli, and, getting ominously and rapidly worse,
was removed from his transport to a French hospital
ship, where, irreproachably cared for, he died in
a few hours and without coming to consciousness.
I deny myself any further anticipation of the story
to which further noble associations attach, and
the merest outline of which indeed tells it and rounds
it off absolutely as the right harmony would have
it. It is perhaps even a touch beyond any dreamt-
of harmony that, under omission of no martial
honour, he was to be carried by comrades and devoted waiting sharers, whose evidence survives
them, to the steep summit of a Greek island of
infinite grace and there placed in such earth and
amid such beauty of light and shade and embracing
prospect as that the fondest reading of his young
lifetime could have suggested nothing better. It
struck us at home, I mean, as symbolising with the
last refinement his whole instinct of selection and
response, his relation to the overcharged appeal
of his scene and hour. How could he have shown
more the young English poetic possibility and
faculty in which we were to seek the freshest re-

flection of the intelligence and the soul of the new generation ? The generosity, I may fairly say the joy, of his contribution to the general perfect way makes a monument of his high rest there at the heart of all that was once noblest in history.

HENRY JAMES

I
ARRIVAL

I

ARRIVAL

HOWEVER sedulously he may have avoided a
preparatory reading of those ' impressions '
of America which our hurried and observant
Great continually record for the instruction
of both nations, the pilgrim who is crossing
the Atlantic for the first time cannot approach
Sandy Hook Bar with so completely blank a
mind as he would wish.   So, at least, I found.
It is not so much that the recent American
invasion of London music-halls has bitten
into one's brain a very definite taste of a
jerking, vital, *bizarre* ' rag-time ' civilisation.
But the various and vivid comments of
friends to whom the news of a traveller's
departure is broken excite and predispose
the imagination.   That so many people who
have been there should have such different
and decided opinions about it !   It must be
at least remarkable.   I felt the thrill of an
explorer before I started.   " A country without conversation," said a philosopher.   " The

big land has a big heart," wrote a kindly
scholar ; and, by the same post, from another
critic, " that land of crushing hospitality ! "
" It's Hell, but it's fine," an artist told me.
" El Cuspidorado," remarked an Oxford man,
brilliantly. But one wiser than all the rest
wrote : " Think gently of the Americans.
They are so very young ; and so very anxious
to appear grown-up ; and so very lovable."
This was more generous than the unvarying
comment of ordinary English friends when
they heard of my purpose, " My God ! "
And it was more precise than those nineteen
several Americans, to each of whom I said,
" I am going to visit America," and each of
whom replied, after long reflection, " Wal !
it's a great country ! "

Travelling by the ordinary routes, you meet
the American people a week before you meet
America. And my excitement to discover
what, precisely, this nation was *at*, was in-
flamed rather than damped by the attitude
of a charming American youth who crossed
by the same boat. That simplicity that is
not far down in any American was very
beautifully on the delightful surface with him.
The second day out he sidled shyly up to me.
" Of what nationality *are* you ? " he asked.

His face showed bewilderment when he heard.
" I thought all Englishmen had moustaches,"
he said. I told him of the infinite variety,
within the homogeneity, of our race. He did
not listen, but settled down near me with the
eager kindliness of a child. " You know,"
he said, " you'll never understand America.
No, Sir. No Englishman can understand
America. I've been in London. In your
Houses of Parliament there is one door for
peers to go in at, and one for ordinary people.
Did I laugh some when I saw that ? You
bet your, America's not like that. In
America one man's just as good as another.
You'll never understand America." I was
all humility. His theme and his friendliness
fired him. He rose with a splendour which,
I had to confess to myself, England could
never have given to him. " Would you like
to hear me re-cite to you the Declaration of
Independence ? " he asked. And he did.

So it was with a fairly blank mind, and yet
a hope of understanding, or at least of seeing,
something very remarkably fresh, that I woke
to hear we were in harbour; and tumbled out
on deck at six of a fine summer morning to
view a new world. New York Harbour is
loveliest at night perhaps. On the Staten

Island ferry boat you slip out from the darkness right under the immense sky-scrapers. As they recede they form into a mass together, heaping up one behind another, fire-lined and majestic, sentinel over the black, gold-streaked waters.   Their cliff-like boldness is the greater, because to either side sweep in the East River and the Hudson River, leaving this piled promontory between.   To the right hangs the great stretch of the Brooklyn Suspension Bridge, its slight curve very purely outlined with light;   over it luminous trams, like shuttles of fire, are thrown across and across, continually weaving the stuff of human existence.   From further off all these lights dwindle to a radiant semicircle that gazes out over the expanse with a quiet, mysterious expectancy.   Far away seaward you may see the low golden glare of Coney Island.

But there was beauty in the view that morning, also, half an hour after sunrise. New York, always the cleanest and least smoky of cities, lay asleep in a queer, pearly, hourless light.   A thin mist softened the further outlines.   The water was opalescent under a silver sky, cool and dim, very slightly ruffled by the sweet wind that followed us in from the sea.   A few streamers of smoke flew above the city, oblique and parallel, pennants of our civilisation. The space of water is great, and so the vast buildings do not tower above one as they do from the street. Scale is lost, and they might be any size. The impression is, rather, of long, low buildings stretching down to the water's edge on every side, and innumerable low black wharves and jetties and piers. And at one point, the lower end of the island on which the city proper stands, rose that higher clump of the great buildings, the Singer, the Woolworth, and the rest. Their strength, almost severity, of line and the lightness of their colour gave a kind of classical feeling, classical, and yet not of Europe. It had the air, this block of masonry, of edifices built to satisfy some faith, for more than immediate ends. Only, the faith was unfamiliar. But if these buildings embodied its nature, it is cold and hard and light, like the steel that is their heart. The first sight of these strange fanes has queer resemblances to the first sight of that lonely and secret group by Pisa's walls. It came upon me, at that moment, that they could not have been dreamed and made without some nobility. Perhaps the hour lent them sanctity. For I have often noticed since

that in the early morning, and again for a
little about sunset, the sky-scrapers are no
longer merely the means and local convenience
for men to pursue their purposes, but acquire
that characteristic of the great buildings of
the world, an existence and meaning of their
own.

Our boat moved up the harbour and along
the Hudson River with a superb and courteous
stateliness. Round her snorted and scuttled
and · puffed the multitudinous strange deni-
zens of the harbour. Tugs, steamers, queer-
shaped ferry-boats, long rafts carrying great
lines of trucks from railway to railway,
dredgers, motor-boats, even a sailing-boat or
two ; for the day's work was beginning.
Among them, with that majesty that only a
liner entering a harbour has, she went, progressed, had her moving—English contains
no word for such a motion—" *incessu patuit
dea.*" A goddess entering fairyland, I thought ;
for the huddled beauty of these buildings and
the still, silver expanse of the water seemed
unreal. Then I looked down at the water
immediately beneath me, and knew that
New York was a real city. All kinds of refuse
went floating by : bits of wood, straw from
barges, bottles, boxes, paper, occasionally a

dead cat or dog, hideously bladder-like, its
four paws stiff and indignant towards heaven.

This analysis of fairyland turned me towards the statue of Liberty, already passed
and growing distant. It is one of those
things you have long wanted to see and
haven't expected to admire, which, seen,
give you a double thrill, that they're at last
there, and that they're better than your hopes.
For Liberty stands nobly. Americans, always
shy about their country, have learnt from the
ridicule which Europeans, on mixed æsthetic
and moral grounds, pour on this statue, to
dismiss it with an apologetic laugh. Yet it
is fine—until you get near enough to see its
clumsiness. I admired the great gesture of
it. A hand fell on my shoulder, and a voice
said, " Look hard at that, young man !
That's the first time you've seen Liberty—and
it will be the last till you turn your back on
this country again." It was an American
fellow-passenger, one of the tall, thin type of
American, with pale blue eyes of an idealistic,
disappointed expression, and an Indian profile.
The other half of America, personated by a
small, bumptious, eager, brown-faced man, with
a cigar raking at an irritating angle from the
corner of his mouth, joined in with, " Wal !

I should smile, I guess this is the Land of Freedom, anyway." The tall man swung round : " Freedom ! do you call it a free land, where—— " He gave instances of the power of the dollar. The other man kept up the argument by spitting and by asseveration. As the busy little tugs, with rugs on their noses, butted the great liner into her narrow dock, the pessimist launched his last shafts. The short man denied nothing. He drew the cigar from his lips, shot it back with a popping noise into the round hole cigars had worn at the corner of his mouth, and said, " Anyway, it's some country." I was introduced to America.

II
NEW YORK

II

NEW YORK

In five things America excels modern England—fish, architecture, jokes, drinks, and children's clothes. There may be others. Of these I am certain. The jokes and drinks, which curiously resemble each other, are the best. There is a cheerful violence about them; they take their respective kingdoms by storm. All the lesser things one has heard turn out to be delightfully true. The first hour in America proves them. People here talk with an American accent; their teeth are inlaid with gold; the mouths of car-conductors move slowly, slowly, with an oblique oval motion, for they are chewing; pavements are 'sidewalks.' It is all true. . . . But there were other things one expected, though in no precise form. What, for instance, would it be like, the feeling of whatever democracy America has secured?

I landed, rather forlorn, that first morning, on the immense covered wharf where the

Customs mysteries were to be celebrated.
The place was dominated by a large, dirty,
vociferous man, coatless, in a black shirt and
black apron. His mouth and jaw were huge ;
he looked like a caricaturist's Roosevelt.
' Express Company ' was written on his forehead ; labels of a thousand colours, printed
slips, pencils and pieces of string, hung from
his pockets and his hands, were held behind
his ears and in his mouth. I laid my situation and my incompetence before him, and
learnt right where to go and right when to
go there. Then he flung a vast, dingy arm
round my shoulders, and bellowed, " We'll
have your baggage right along to your hotel
in two hours." It was a lie, but kindly. That
grimy and generous embrace left me startled,
but an initiate into Democracy.

The other evening I went a lonely ramble,
to try to detect the essence of New York.
A wary eavesdropper can always surprise the
secret of a city, through chance scraps of
conversation, or by spying from a window, or
by coming suddenly round corners. I started
on a ' car.' American tram-cars are open
all along the side and can be entered at any
point in it. The side is divided by vertical
bars. It looks like a cage with the horizontal

lines taken out. Between these vertical bars you squeeze into the seat. If the seat opposite you is full, you swing yourself along the bars by your hands till you find room. The Americans become terrifyingly expert at this. I have seen them, fat, middle-aged business men, scampering up and down the face of the cars by means of their hands, swinging themselves over and round and above each other, like nothing in the world so much as the monkeys at the Zoo. It is a people informed with vital energy. I believe that this exercise, and the habit of drinking a lot of water between meals, are the chief causes of their good health.

The Broadway car runs mostly along the backbone of the queer island on which this city stands. So the innumerable parallel streets that cross it curve down and away; and at this time street after street to the west reveals, and seems to drop into, a mysterious evening sky, full of dull reds and yellows, amber and pale green, and a few pink flecks, and in the midst, sometimes, the flushed, smoke-veiled face of the sun. Then greyness, broken by these patches of misty colour, settles into the lower channels of the New York streets; while the upper heights of the sky-scrapers, clear of the roofs, are still lit on the sunward side with a mellow glow, curiously serene. To the man in the mirk of the street, they seem to exude this light from the great spaces of brick. At this time the cars, always polyglot, are filled with shop-hands and workers, and no English at all is heard. One is surrounded with Yiddish, Italian, and Greek, broken by Polish, or Russian, or German. Some American anthropologists claim that the children of these immigrants show marked changes, in the shape of skull and face, towards the American type. It may be so. But the people who surround one are mostly European-born. They represent very completely that H.C.F. of Continental appearance which is labelled in the English mind 'looking like a foreigner'; being short, swarthy, gesticulatory, full of clatter, indeterminately alien. Only in their dress and gait have they—or at least the men among them—become at all American.

The American by race walks better than we ; more freely, with a taking swing, and almost with grace. How much of this is due to living in a democracy, and how much to wearing no braces, it is very difficult to determine. But certainly it is the land of

belts, and therefore of more loosely moving
bodies. This, and the padded shoulders of
the coats, and the loosely-cut trousers, make
a figure more presentable, at a distance, than
most urban civilisations turn out. Also,
Americans take their coats off, which is
sensible; and they can do it the more beautifully because they are belted, and not braced.
They take their coats off anywhere and any-
when, and somehow it strikes the visitor as
the most symbolic thing about them. They
have not yet thought of discarding collars;
but they are unashamedly shirt-sleeved. Any
sculptor, seeking to figure this Republic in
stone, must carve, in future, a young man in
shirt-sleeves, open-faced, pleasant, and rather
vulgar, straw hat on the back of his head,
his trousers full and sloppy, his coat over his
arm. The motto written beneath will be, of
course, 'This is some country.' The philo-
sophic gazer on such a monument might get
some way towards understanding the making
of the Panama Canal, that exploit that no
European nation could have carried out.

What facial type the sculptor would give
the youth is harder to determine, and very
hard to describe. The American race seems
to have developed two classes, and only two,

the upper-middle and the lower-middle. Their
faces are very distinct. The upper-class head
is long, often fine about the forehead and eyes,
and very cleanly outlined. The eyes have
an odd, tired pathos in them—mixed with the
friendliness that is so admirable—as if of a
perpetual never quite successful effort to
understand something. It is like the face
of an only child who has been brought up in
the company of adults. I am convinced it
is partly due to the endeavour to set their
standards by the culture and traditions of
older nations. But the mouth of such men
is the most typical feature. It is small, tight,
and closed downwards at the corners, the
lower lip very slightly protruding. It has
little expression in it, and no curves. There
the Puritan comes out. But no other nation
has a mouth like this. It is shared to some
extent by the lower classes; but their mouths
tend to be wider and more expressive. Their
foreheads are meaner, and their eyes hard,
but the whole face rather more adaptive and
in touch with life. These, anyhow, are the
types that strike one in the Eastern cities.
And there are intermediate varieties, as of
the genial business-man, with the narrow
forehead and the wide, smooth—the too wide

and too smooth—lower face. Smoothness
is the one unfailing characteristic. Why do
American faces hardly ever wrinkle ? Is it
the absence of a soul ? It must be. For it
is less true of the Bostonian than of the
ordinary business American, in whose life
exhilaration and depression take the place of
joy and suffering. The women's faces are
more indeterminate, not very feminine ; many
of them wear those ' invisible ' pince-nez
which centre glitteringly about the bridge
of the nose, and get from them a curious
air of intelligence. Handsome people of both
sexes are very common ; beautiful, and pretty,
ones very rare. . . .

I slipped from my car up about Fortieth
Street, the region where the theatres and
restaurants are, the ' roaring forties.' Broadway here might be the offspring of Shaftesbury
Avenue and Leicester Square, with, somehow,
some of Fleet Street also in its ancestry. I
passed two men on the sidewalk, their hats
on the back of their heads, arguing fiercely.
One had slightly long hair. The other looked
the more truculent, and was saying to him,
intensely, " See here ! We con—tracted with
you to supply us with sonnets at five dollars
per sonnet—— " I passed up a side-street, one

of those deserted ways that abound just
off the big streets, resorts, apparently, for
such people and things as are not quite
strident or not quite energetic enough for the
ordinary glare of life ; dim places, fusty with
hesternal excitements and the thrills of yester-
year. Against a flight of desolate steps leant
a notice. I stopped to read it. It said :

> "You must see Cockie,
> Positively the only bird that can both dance and sing.
> She is almost superhuman."

There was no explanation ; Cockie may have
been dead for years. I went, musing on her
possible fates, towards the pride and spacious-
ness of Fifth Avenue.

Fifth Avenue is handsome, the handsomest
street imaginable. It is what the streets
of German cities try to be. The buildings
are large, square, ' imposing,' built with the
solidity of opulence. The street, as a whole,
has a character and an air of achievement.
"Whatever else may be doubted or denied,
American civilisation has produced this." One
feels rich and safe as one walks. Back in
Broadway, New York dropped her mask, and
began to betray herself once again. A little
crowd, expressionless, intent, and volatile,

before a small shop, drew me. In the shop-window was a young man, pleasant-faced, a little conscious, and a little bored, dressed very lightly in what might have been a runner's costume. He was bowing, twisting, and posturing in a slow rhythm. From time to time he would put a large card on a little stand in the corner. The cards bore various legends. He would display a card that said, " THIS UNDERWEAR DOES NOT IMPEDE THE MOVEMENT OF THE BODY IN ANY DIRECTION." Then he moved his body in every direction, from position to position, probable or improbable, and was not impeded. With a terrible dumb patience he turned the next card : " IT GIVES WITH THE BODY IN VIOLENT EXERCISING." The young man leapt suddenly, lunged, smote imaginary balls, belaboured invisible opponents, ran with immense speed but no progress, was thrown to earth by the Prince of the Air, kicked, struggled, then bounded to his feet again. But all this without a word. " IT ENABLES YOU TO KEEP COOL WHILE EXERCISING." The young man exercised, and yet was cool. He did this, I discovered later, for many hours a day.

Not daring to imagine his state of mind, I hurried off through Union Square. One of the many daily fire-alarms had gone; the traffic was drawn to one side, and several fire-engines came, with clanging of bells and shouting, through the space, gleaming with brass, splendid in their purpose. Before the thrill in the heart had time to die, or the traffic to close up, swung through an immense open motor-car driven by a young mechanic. It was luxuriously appointed, and had the air of a private car being returned from repairing. The man in it had an almost Swinburnian mane of red hair, blowing back in the wind, catching the last lights of day. He was clad, as such people often are in this country these hot days, only in a suit of yellow overalls, so that his arms and shoulders and neck and chest were bare. He was big, well-made, and strong, and he drove the car, not wildly, but a little too fast, leaning back rather insolently conscious of power. In private life, no doubt, a very ordinary youth, interested only in baseball scores; but in this brief passage he seemed like a Greek god, in a fantastically modern, yet not unworthy way emblemed and incarnate, or like the spirit of Henley's ' Song of Speed.' So I found a better image of America for my sculptor than the shirt-sleeved young man.

III
NEW YORK

III

NEW YORK (*continued*)

THE hotel into which the workings of blind chance have thrown me is given over to commercial travellers. Its life is theirs, and the few English tourists creep in and out with the shy, bewildered dignity of their race and class. These American commercial travellers are called ' drummers '; drummers in the most endless and pointless and extraordinary of wars. They have the air and appearance of devotees, men set aside, roaming preachers of a *jehad* whose meaning they have forgotten. They seem to be invariably of the short, dark type. The larger, fair-haired, long-headed men are common in business, but not in ' drumming.' The drummer's eyes have a hard, rapt expression. He is not interested in the romance of the road, like an English commercial traveller; only in its ever-changing end. These people are for ever sending off and receiving telegrams, messages, and cablegrams; they are continually telephoning;

stenographers are in waiting to record their inspirations. In the intervals of activity they relapse into a curious trance, husbanding their vitality for the next crisis. I have watched them with terror and fascination. All day there are numbers of them sitting, immote and vacant, in rows and circles on the hard chairs in the hall. They are never smoking, never reading a paper, never even chewing. The expressions of their faces never change. It is impossible to guess what, or if anything, is in their minds. Hour upon hour they remain. Occasionally one will rise, in obedience to some call or revelation incomprehensible to us, and move out through the door into the clang and confusion of Broadway.

It all confirms the impression that grows on the visitor to America that Business has developed insensibly into a Religion, in more than the light, metaphorical sense of the words. It has its ritual and theology, its high places and its jargon, as well as its priests and martyrs. One of its more mystical mani-festations is in advertisement. America has a childlike faith in advertising. They adver-tise here, everywhere, and in all ways. They shout your most private and sacred wants at you. Nothing is untouched. Every day I

pass a wall, some five hundred square feet of
which a gentleman has taken to declare that
he is ' out ' to break the Undertakers' Trust.
Half the advertisement is a coloured photograph of himself. The rest is, " See what I
give you for 75 dols. ! " and a list of what
he does give. He gives everything that
the most morbid taphologist could suggest,
beginning with " splendidly carved full-size
oak casket, with black ivory handles. ˙ Four
drapèd Flambeaux . . . " and going on to
funereal ingenuities that would have over-
whelmed Mausolus, and make death impossible for a refined man.

But there are heights as well as depths.
I have been privileged with some intimate
glances into the greatest of those peculiarly
American institutions, the big departmental
stores. Materially it is an immense building,
containing all things that any upper-middle-
class person could conceivably want. Such a
store includes even Art, with the same bland
omnipotence. If you wander into the vast
auditorium, it is equal chances whether you
hear a work of Beethoven, Victor Herbert,
Schonberg, or Mr Hirsch. If you are ' artistic,'
you may choose between a large coloured
photograph of the Eiffel Tower, a carbon

print of Botticelli, and a reproduction of an
'improvisation' by Herr Kandinsky. You
may buy an Elizabethan dining-table, a
Græco-Roman bronze, the latest dress de-
signed by M. Bakst, or a packet of pins. Or
you may sit and muse on the life of the
employee of this place, who gets from it
all that in less favoured civilisations family,
guild, club, township, and nationality have
given him or her. As a child he gets
education, then evening-classes, continuation-
schools, gymnasia, military training, swim-
ming-baths, orchestra, facilities for the study
of anything under the sun, from palæography
to Cherokee, libraries, holiday-camps, hospitals,
ever-present medical attendance, and at the
end a pension, and, I suppose, a store cemetery.
And all for the price of a few hours' work a
day, and a little loyalty to the 'establishment.'
Can human hearts desire more ? And, when
all millionaires are as sensible, will they ?
In industries and businesses like this, where
the majority of the employed are women, it
ought to be a pretty stable sort of millennium.
Men, perhaps, take longer to learn that kind
of 'loyalty.'

In one corner of this store is the advertising department. There are gathered poets,

artists, *littérateurs*, and mere intellectuals, all engaged in explaining to the upper middle-classes what there is for them to buy and why they should buy it. It is a life of good salary, steady hours, sufficient leisure, and entire dignity. There is no vulgarity in this advertising, but the most perfect taste and great artistic daring and novelty. The most ' advanced ' productions of Europe are scanned for ideas and suggestions. Two of the leading young ' post-impressionist ' painters in Paris, whose names are just beginning to be known in England, have been designing posters for this store for years. I stood and watched with awe a young American genius doing entirely Matisse-like illustrations to some notes on summer suitings. " We give our artists a free hand," said the very intelligent lady in charge of that section ; ' except, of course, for nudes or improprieties. And we don't allow any figures of people *smoking*. Some of our customers object very strongly..."

Cities, like cats, will reveal themselves at night. There comes an hour of evening when lower Broadway, the business end of the town, is deserted. And if, having felt yourself immersed in men and the frenzy of cities all day, you stand out in the street in this sudden hush, you will hear, like a strange questioning voice from another world, the melancholy boom of a foghorn, and realise that not half a mile away are the waters of the sea, and some great liner making its slow way out to the Atlantic. After that, the lights come out up-town, and the New York of theatres and vaudevilles and restaurants begins to roar and flare. The merciless lights throw a mask of unradiant glare on the human beings in the streets, making each face hard, set, wolfish, terribly blue. The chorus of voices becomes shriller. The buildings tower away into obscurity, looking strangely theatrical, because lit from below. And beyond them soars the purple roof of the night. A stranger of another race, loitering here, might cast his eyes up, in a vague wonder what powers, kind or maleficent, controlled or observed this whirlpool. He would find only this unresponsive canopy of black, unpierced even, if the seeker stood near a centre of lights, by any star. But while he looks, away up in the sky, out of the gulfs of night, spring two vast fiery tooth-brushes, erect, leaning towards each other, and hanging on to the bristles of them a little Devil, little but gigantic, who kicks and wriggles and glares. After a few moments the Devil, baffled by the firmness of the bristles, stops, hangs still, rolls his eyes, moon-large, and, in a fury of disappointment, goes out, leaving only the night, blacker and a little bewildered, and the unconscious throngs of ant-like human beings. Turning with terrified relief from this exhibition of diabolic impotence, the stranger finds a divine hand writing slowly across the opposite quarter of the heavens its igneous message of warning to the nations, " Wear —— Underwear for Youths and Men-Boys." And close by this message come forth a youth and a man-boy, flaming and immortal, clad in celestial underwear, box a short round, vanish, reappear for another round, and again disappear. Night after night they wage this combat. What gods they are who fight endlessly and indecisively over New York is not for our knowledge ; whether it be Thor and Odin, or Zeus and Cronos, or Michael and Lucifer, or Ormuzd and Ahriman, or Good-as-a-means and Good-as-an-end. The ways of our lords were ever riddling and obscure. To the right a celestial bottle, stretching from the horizon to the zenith, appears, is uncorked, and scatters the worlds with the foam of what ambrosial liquor may have been within.   Beyond, a Spanish goddess, some minor deity in the Dionysian theogony, dances continually, rapt and mysterious, to the music of the spheres, her head in Cassiopeia and her twinkling feet among the Pleiades. And near her, Orion, archer no longer, releases himself from his strained posture to drive a sidereal golf-ball out of sight through the meadows of Paradise ; then poses, addresses, and drives again.

> " O Nineveh, are these thy gods,
>   Thine also, mighty Nineveh ? "

Why this theophany, or how the gods have got out to perform their various ' stunts ' on the *flammantia mœnia mundi*, is not asked by their incurious devotees.   Through Broadway the dingily glittering tide spreads itself over the sands of ' amusement.' Theatres and ' movies ' are aglare. Cars shriek down the street ; the Elevated train clangs and curves perilously overhead ; newsboys wail the baseball news ; wits cry their obscure challenges to one another, ' I should worry ! ' or ' She's some Daisy ! ' or ' Good-night, Nurse ! ' In houses off the streets around children are being born, lovers are kissing, people are dying. Above, in the midst of those coruscating divinities, sits one older and greater than any. Most colossal of all, it flashes momently out, a woman's head, all flame against the darkness. It is beautiful, passionless, in its simplicity and conventional representation queerly like an archaic Greek or early Egyptian figure. Queen of the night behind, and of the gods around, and of the city below—here, if at all, you think, may one find the answer to the riddle. Her ostensible message, burning in the firmament beside her, is that we should buy pepsin chewing-gum. But there is more, not to be given in words, ineffable. Suddenly, when she has surveyed mankind, she closes her left eye. Three times she winks, and then vanishes. No ordinary winks these, but portentous, terrifyingly steady, obliterating a great tract of the sky. Hour by hour she does this, night by night, year by year. That enigmatic obscuration of light, that answer that is no answer, is, perhaps, the first thing in this world that a child born near here will see, and the last that a dying man will have to take for a message to the curious dead She is immortal. Men have worshipped her as Isis and as Ashtaroth, as Venus, as Cybele, Mother of the Gods, and as Mary. There is

a statue of her by the steps of the British
Museum.   Here, above the fantastic civilisation she observes, she has no name. , She is
older than the sky-scrapers amongst which
she sits ; and one, certainly, of her eyelids is
a trifle weary.   And the only answer to our
cries, the only comment upon our cities, is
that divine stare, the wink, once, twice, thrice.
And then darkness.

IV

BOSTON AND HARVARD

IV

BOSTON AND HARVARD

It is right to leave Boston late in a summer
afternoon, and by sea. Naval departure is
always the better. A train snatches you,
hot, dusty, and smoky, with an irritated
hurry out of the back parts of a town. The
last glimpse of a place you may have grown
to like or love is, ignobly, interminable rows
of the bedroom-windows in mean streets, a
few hovels, some cinder-heaps, and a factory
chimney. As like as not, you are reft from
a last wave to the city's unresponsive and
dingy back by the roar and suffocation of a
tunnel. By sea one takes a gracefuller, more
satisfactory farewell.

Boston put on her best appearance to
watch our boat go out for New York. The
harbour was bright with sunlight and blue
water and little white sails, and there wasn't
more than the faintest smell of tea. The
city sat primly on her little hills, decorous,
civilised, European-looking. It is homely after

New York. The Boston crowd is curiously
English. They have nice eighteenth-century
houses there, and ivy grows on the buildings.
And they are hospitable. All Americans are
hospitable ; but they haven't *quite* time in
New York to practise the art so perfectly as
the Bostonians. It is a lovely art. . . . But
Boston also makes you feel at home without
meaning to. A delicious ancient Toryism is
to be found here. " What is wrong with
America," a middle-aged lady told me, " is
this *Democracy.* They ought to take the
votes away from these people, who don't
know how to use them, and give them only
to *us,* the Educated." My heart leapt the
Atlantic, and was in a Cathedral or University
town of South England.

Yet Boston is alive. It sits, in comfortable
middle-age, on the ruins of its glory. But it
is not buried beneath them. It used to lead
America in Literature, Thought, Art, everything. The years have passed. It is remarkable how nearly now Boston is to New
York what Munich is to Berlin. Boston and
Munich were the leaders forty years ago.
They can't quite make out that they aren't
now. It is too incredible that Art should
leave her goose-feather bed and away to the

wraggle-taggle business-men. And certainly,
if Berlin and New York are more ' live,'
Boston and Munich are more themselves, less
feverishly imitations of Paris. But the un-
disputed palm is there no more ; and its
absence is felt.

But I had little time to taste Boston itself.
I was lured across the river to a place called
Cambridge, where is the University of Harvard.
Harvard is the Oxford and Cambridge of
America, they claim. She has moulded the
nation's leaders and uttered its ideals. Harvard, Boston, New England, it is impossible to
say how much they are interwoven, and how
they have influenced America. I saw Harvard
in ' Commencement,' which is Eights Week
and May Week, the festive winding-up of the
year, a time of parties and of valedictions.
One of the great events of Commencement,
and of the year, is the Harvard-Yale baseball
match. To this I went, excited at the prospect of my first sight of a ' ball game,' and
my mind vaguely reminiscent of the indolent,
decorous, upper-class crowd, the sunlit spaces,
the dignified ritual, and white-flannelled grace
of Lord's at the 'Varsity cricket match. The
crowd was gay, and not very large. We sat
in wooden stands, which were placed in the

shape of a large V. As all the hitting which counts in baseball takes place well in front of the wicket, so to speak, the spectators have the game right under their noses ; the striker stands in the angle of the V and plays outwards. The field was a vast place, partly stubbly grass, partly worn and patchy, like a parade-ground. Beyond it lay the river ; beyond that the town of Cambridge and the University buildings. Around me were undergraduates, with their mothers and sisters. ' Cambridge ' ! . . . but there entered to us, across the field, a troop of several hundred men, all dressed in striped shirts of the same hue and pattern, and headed by a vast banner which informed the world that they were the graduates of 1910, celebrating their triennial. In military formation they moved across the plain towards us, led by a band, ceaselessly vociferating, and raising their straw hats in unison to mark the time. There followed the class of 1907, attired as sailors ; 1908, the decennial class, with some samples of their male children marching with them, and a banner inscribed " 515 Others. No Race Suicide " ; 1898, carefully arranged in an H-shaped formation, dancing along to their music with a slow polka-step, each with his

hands on the shoulders of the man in front,
and at the head of all their leader, dancing
backwards in perfect time, marshalling them ;
1888, middle-aged men, again with some
children, and a Highland regiment playing
the bagpipes.

When these had passed to the seats allotted
for them, I had time to observe the players,
who were practising about the ground, and I
was shocked. They wear dust-coloured shirts
and dingy knickerbockers, fastened under the
knee, and heavy boots. They strike the
English eye as being attired for football, or
a gladiatorial combat, rather than a summer
game. The very close-fitting caps, with large
peaks, give them picturesquely the appearance
of hooligans. Baseball is a good game to
watch, and in outline easy to understand, as
it is merely glorified rounders. A cricketer is
fascinated by their rapidity and skill in catching and throwing. There is excitement in
the game, but little beauty except in the
long-limbed ' pitcher,' whose duty it is to
hurl the ball rather further than the length
of a cricket-pitch, as bewilderingly as possible.
In his efforts to combine speed, mystery,
and curve, he gets into attitudes of a very
novel and fantastic, but quite obvious,

beauty. M. Nijinsky would find them repay study.

One queer feature of this sport is that un-occupied members of the batting side, fielders, and even spectators, are accustomed to join in vocally. You have the spectacle of the representatives of the universities endeavouring to frustrate or unnerve their opponents, at moments of excitement, by cries of derision and mockery, or heartening their own supporters and performers with exclamations of 'Now, Joe!' or 'He's got them!' or 'He's the boy!' At the crises in the fortunes of the game, the spectators take a collective and important part. The Athletic Committee appoints a 'cheer-leader' for the occasion. Every five or ten minutes this gentleman, a big, fine figure in white, springs out from his seat at the foot of the stands, addresses the multitude through a megaphone with a 'One! Two! Three!' hurls it aside, and, with a wild flinging and swinging of his body and arms, conducts ten thousand voices in the Harvard yell. That over, the game proceeds, and the cheer-leader sits quietly waiting for the next moment of peril or triumph. I shall not easily forget that figure, bright in the sunshine, conducting with his whole body,

passionate, possessed by a demon, bounding
in the frenzy of his inspiration from side to
side, contorted, rhythmic, ecstatic. It seemed
so wonderfully American, in its combination
of entire wildness and entire regulation, with
the whole just a trifle fantastic. Completely
friendly and befriended as I was, I couldn't
help feeling at those moments very alien and
very, very old—even more so than after the
protracted game had ended in a victory for
Harvard, when the dusty plain was filled with
groups and lines of men dancing in solemn
harmony, and a shouting crowd, broken by
occasional individuals who could find some
little eminence to lead a Harvard yell from,
and who conducted the bystanders, and then
vanished, and the crowd swirled on again.

Different enough was the scene next day,
when all Harvard men who were up for Commencement assembled and, arranged by years,
marched round the yard. Class by class they
paraded, beginning with veterans of the
'fifties, down to the class of 1912. I wonder
if English nerves could stand it. It seems
to bring the passage of time so very presently
and vividly to the mind. To see, with such
emphatic regularity, one's coevals changing
in figure, and diminishing in number, summer

after summer ! . . . Perhaps it is nobler,
this deliberate viewing of oneself as part of
the stream. To the spectator, certainly, the
flow and transiency become apparent and
poignant. In five minutes fifty years of
America, of so much of America, go past one.
The shape of the bodies, apart from the
effects of age, the lines of the faces, the ways
of wearing hair and beard and moustaches, all
these change a little decade by decade, before
your eyes. And through the whole appearance runs some continuity, which is Harvard.

The orderly progression of the years was
unbroken, except at one point. There was
one gap, large and arresting. Though all
years were represented, there seemed to be
nobody in the procession between fifty and
sixty. I asked a Harvard friend the reason.
" The War," he said. He told me there had
always been that gap. Those who were old
enough to be conscious of the war had lost
a big piece of their lives. With their suc-
cessors a new America began. I don't know
how true it is. Certainly, the dates worked out
right. And I met an American on a boat who
had been a child in one of the neutral States.
He used to watch the regiments forming in the
main street of his town, and marching out, some

north and some south. He said it felt as though
pieces of his body were being torn in different
directions. And he was only nine.

The procession filed in to an open court, to
hear the speeches of the recipients of honorary
degrees, and the President's annual statement.
There was still, in every sense, a solemn
atmosphere. The President's speech floated
out into the great open space ; fragments of it
were blown to one's ears concerning deaths, and
the spirit of the place, and a detailed account
of the money given during the year. Eleven
hundred thousand dollars in all—a record,
or nearly a record. We roared applause. The
American universities appear still to dream of
the things of this world. They keep putting up
the most wonderful and expensive buildings.
But they do not pay their teachers well.

Yet Harvard is a spirit, a way of looking at
things, austerely refined, gently moral, kindly.
The perception of it grows on the foreigner.
Its charm is so deliciously old in this land, so
deliciously young compared with the lovely
frowst of Oxford and Cambridge. You see it
in temperament, the charm of simplicity and
good-heartedness and culture ; in the Harvard
undergraduate, who is a boy, while his English
contemporary is either a young man or a

schoolboy, less pleasant stages ; and in the old Bostonian who heard, and still hears, the lectures of Dickens and Thackeray. Class Day brings so many of that older generation together. They reveal what Harvard, what Boston, was. There is something terrifying in the completeness of their lives and their civilisation. They are like a company of dons whose studies are of a remote and finished world. But the subject of their scholarship is the Victorian age, and especially Victorian England. Hence their liveliness and certainty, greater than men can reach who are concerned with the dubieties and changes of incomplete things. Hence the wit, the stock of excellent stories, the wrinkled wisdom and mirth of the type. They are the flower of a civilisation, its ripest critics, and final judges. Carlyle and Emerson are their greatest living heroes. One of them bent the kindliness and alert interest of his eighty years upon me. " So you come from Rugby," he said. " Tell me, do you know that curious creature, Matthew Arnold ? " I couldn't bring myself to tell him that, even in Rugby, we had forgiven that brilliant youth his iconoclastic tendencies some time since, and that, as a matter of fact, he had died when I was eight months old.

V

MONTREAL AND OTTAWA

MONTREAL AND OTTAWA

My American friends were full of kindly
scorn when I announced that I was going to
Canada. 'A country without a soul!' they
cried, and pressed books upon me, to befriend
me through that Philistine bleakness. Their
commiseration unnerved me, but I was
heartened by a feeling that I was, in a sense,
going home, and by the romance of journeying.
There was romance in the long grim American
train, in the great lake we passed in the
blackest of nights, and could just see glinting
behind dark trees; in the negro car-attendant;
in the boy who perpetually cried : ' Pea-nuts !
Candy !' up and down the long carriages;
in the lofty box they put me in to sleep; and
in the fat old lady who had the berth under
mine, and snored shrilly the whole night
through. There was almost romance, even, in
the fact that after all there was no restaurant-
car on the train; and, having walked all day
in the country, I dined off an orange.

I suppose an Englishman in another country, if he is simple enough, is continually and alternately struck by two thoughts : ' How like England this is ! ' and ' How unlike England this is ! ' When I had woken next morning, and, lying on my back, had got inside my clothes with a series of fish-like jumps, I found myself looking with startled eyes out of the window at the largest river I had ever seen. It was blue, and sunlit, and it curved spaciously. But beyond that we ran into the squalider parts of a city. It became immediately obvious that we were not in New York or Boston or any of the more orderly, the rather foreign, cities of America. There was something in the untidiness of those grimy houses, the smoky disorder of the backyards, that ran a thrill of nostalgia through me. I recognised the English way of doing things—with a difference that I could not define till later.

Determined to be in all ways the complete tourist, I took a rough preliminary survey of Montreal in an ' observation-car.' It was a large motor-wagonette, from which everything in Montreal could be seen in two hours. We were a most fortuitous band of twenty, who had elected so to see it. Our guide addressed us from the front through a small megaphone, telling us what everything was, what we were to be interested in, what to overlook, what to admire. He seemed the exact type of a spiritual pastor and master, shepherding his stolid and perplexed flock on a regulated path through the dust and clatter of the world. And the great hollow device out of which our instruction proceeded was so perfectly a blind mouth. I had never understood *Lycidas* before. We were sheepish enough, and fairly hungry. However, we were excellently fed. " On the right, ladies and gentlemen, is the Bank of Montreal; on the left the Presbyterian Church of St Andrew's; on the right, again, the well-designed residence of Sir Blank Blank ; further on, on the same side, the Art Museum. . . ." The outcome of it all was a vague general impression that Montreal consists of banks and churches. The people of this city spend much of their time in laying up their riches in this world or the next. Indeed, the British part of Montreal is dominated by the Scotch race ; there is a Scotch spirit sensible in the whole place—in the rather narrow, rather gloomy streets, the solid, square, grey, aggressively prosperous buildings, the general greyness of the city, the air of dour prosperity. Even the Canadian habit of loading the streets with heavy telephone wires, supported by frequent black poles, seemed to increase the atmospheric resemblance to Glasgow.

But besides all this there is a kind of restraint in the air, due, perhaps, to a state of affairs which, more than any other, startles the ordinary ignorant English visitor. The average man in England has an idea of Canada as a young-eyed daughter State, composed of millions of wheat-growers and backwoodsmen of British race. It surprises him to learn that more than a quarter of the population is of French descent, that many of them cannot speak English, that they control a province, form the majority in the biggest city in Canada, and are a perpetual complication in the national politics. Even a stranger who knows this is startled at the complete separateness of the two races. Inter-marriage is very rare. They do not meet socially; only on business, and that not often. In the same city these two communities dwell side by side, with different traditions, different languages, different ideals, without sympathy or comprehension. The French in Canada are entirely devoted to—some say under the thumb of—the Roman Catholic Church. They seem like a piece of the Middle Ages, dumped after a trans-secular journey into a quite uncompromising example of our commercial time. Some of their leaders are said to have dreams of a French Republic—or theocracy—on the banks of the St Lawrence. How this, or any other, solution of the problem is to come about, no man knows. Racial difficulties are the most enduring of all. The French and British in Canada seem to have behaved with quite extraordinary generosity and kindliness towards each other. No one is to blame. But it is not in human nature that two communities should live side by side, pretending they are one, without some irritation and mutual loss of strength. There is no open strife. But 'incidents,' and the memory of incidents, bear continual witness to the truth of the situation. And racial disagreement is at the bottom, often unconsciously, of many political and social movements. Sir Wilfrid Laurier performed a miracle. But no one of French birth will ever again be Premier of Canada.

Montreal and Eastern Canada suffer from that kind of ill-health which afflicts men who are cases of 'double personality'—debility and spiritual paralysis. The 'progressive'

British-Canadian man of commerce is comically desperate of peasants who *will not* understand that increase of imports and volume of trade and numbers of millionaires are the measures of a city's greatness; and to his eye the Roman Catholic Church, with her invaluable ally Ignorance, keeps up her incessant war against the general good of the community of which she is part. So things remain.

I made my investigations in Montreal. I have to report that the Discobolus[1] is very well, and, nowadays, looks the whole world in the face, almost quite unabashed. West of Montreal, the country seems to take on a rather more English appearance. There is still a French admixture. But the little houses are not purely Gallic, as they are along the Lower St Lawrence; and orce or twice I detected real hedges.

Ottawa came as a relief after Montreal. There is no such sense of strain and tightness in the atmosphere. The British, if not greatly in the majority, are in the ascendency; also, the city seems conscious of other than financial standards, and quietly, with dignity, aware of her own purpose. The Canadians, like the Americans, chose to have for their capital a

---

[1] See Samuel Butler's poem, "Oh God! oh Montreal!"—ED.

city which did not lead in population or in wealth. This is particularly fortunate in Canada, an extremely individualistic country, whose inhabitants are only just beginning to be faintly conscious of their nationality. Here, at least, Canada is more than the Canadian. A man desiring to praise Ottawa would begin to do so without statistics of wealth and the growth of population; and this can be said of no other city in Canada except Quebec. Not that there are not immense lumber-mills and the rest in Ottawa. But the Government farm, and the Parliament buildings, are more important. Also, although the ' spoils ' system obtains a good deal in this country, the nucleus of the Civil Service is much the same as in England; so there is an atmosphere of Civil Servants about Ottawa, an atmosphere of safeness and honour and massive buildings and well-shaded walks. After all, there is in the qualities of Civility and Service much beauty, of a kind which would adorn Canada.

Parliament Buildings stand finely on a headland of cliff some 160 feet above the river. There are gardens about them; and beneath, the wooded rocks go steeply down to the water. It is a position of natural boldness and significance. The buildings were put up in the middle of last century, an unfortunate period. But they have dignity, especially of line; and when evening hides their colour, and the western sky and the river take on the lovely hues of a Canadian sunset, and the lights begin to come out in the city, they seem to have the majesty and calm of a natural crown of the river-headland. The Government have bought the ground along the cliff for half a mile on either side, and propose to build all their offices there. So, in the end, if they build well, the river-front at Ottawa will be a noble sight. And—just to show that it is Canada, and not Utopia—the line of national buildings will always be broken by an expensive and superb hotel the Canadian Pacific Railway has been allowed to erect on the twin and neighbouring promontory to that of the Houses of Parliament.

The streets of Ottawa are very quiet, and shaded with trees. The houses are mostly of that cool, homely, wooden kind, with verandahs, on which, or on the steps, the whole family may sit in the evening and observe the passers-by. This is possible for both the rich and the poor, who live nearer each other in Ottawa than in most cities. In general there is an air of civilisation, which extends even over the country round. But in the country you see little signs, a patch of swamp, or thickets of still untouched primæval wood, which remind you that Europeans have not long had this land. I was taken in a motor-car some twenty miles or more over the execrable roads round here, to a lovely little lake in the hills north-west of Ottawa. We went by little French villages and fields at first, and then through rocky, tangled woods of birch and poplar, rich with milk-weed and blue cornflowers, and the aromatic thimble-berry blossom, and that romantic, light, purple-red flower which is called fireweed, because it is the first vegetation to spring up in the prairie after a fire has passed over, and so might be adopted as the emblematic flower of a sense of humour. They told me, casually, that there was nothing but a few villages between me and the North Pole. It is probably true of several commonly frequented places in this country. But it gives a thrill to hear it.

But what Ottawa leaves in the mind is a certain graciousness—dim, for it expresses a barely materialised national spirit—and the sight of kindly English-looking faces, and the rather lovely sound of the soft Canadian accent, in the streets.

VI

QUEBEC AND THE SAGUENAY

VI

QUEBEC AND THE SAGUENAY

THE boat starts from Montreal one evening, and lands you in Quebec at six next morning. The evening I left was a dull one. Heavy sulphurous clouds hung low over the city, drifting very slowly and gloomily out across the river. Mount Royal crouched, black and sullen, in the background, its crest occluded by the darkness, appearing itself a cloud materialised, resting on earth. The harbour was filled with volumes of smoke, purple and black, wreathing and sidling eastwards, from steamers and chimneys. The gigantic elevators and other harbour buildings stood mistily in this inferno, their heads clear and sinister above the mirk. It was impossible to decide whether an enormous mass of pitchy and Tartarian gloom was being slowly moulded by diabolic invisible hands into a city, or a city, the desperate and damned abode of a loveless race, was disintegrating into its proper fume and dusty chaos. With relief we turned outwards to the nobility of the St Lawrence and the gathering dark.

On the boat I fell in with another wanderer, an American Jew, and we joined our fortunes, rather loosely, for a few days. He was one of those men whom it is a life-long pleasure to remember. I can record his existence the more easily that there is not the slightest chance of his ever reading these lines. He was a fat, large man of forty-five, obviously in business, and probably of a mediocre success. His eyes were light-coloured, very small, always watery, and perpetually roving. The lower part of his face was clean-shaven and very broad ; his mouth wide, with thin, moist, colourless lips ; his nose fat and Hebraic. He was rather bald. He had respect for Montreal, because, though closed to navigation for five months in the year, it is the second busiest port on the coast. He said it had Boston skinned. The French he disliked. He thought they stood in the way of Canada's progress. His mind was even more childlike and transparent than is usual with business men. The observer could see thoughts slowly floating into it, like carp in a pond. When they got near the surface, by a purely automatic process they found utterance. He was almost com-

pletely unconscious of an audience. Everything he thought of he said. He told me that
his boots were giving in the sole, but would
probably last this trip. He said he had not
washed his feet for eight days ; and that his
clothes were shabby (which was true), but
would do for Canada. It was interesting to
see how Canada presented herself to that
mind. He seemed to regard her as a kind
of Bœotia, and terrifyingly dour. " These
Canadian waiters," he said, " they jes' *fling*
the food in y'r face. Kind'er gets yer sick,
doesn't it ? " I agreed. There was a York-
shire mechanic, too, who had been in Canada
four years, and preferred it to England, " because you've room to breathe," but also found
that Canada had not yet learnt social comfort, and regretted the manners of " the Old
Country."

We woke to find ourselves sweeping round
a high cliff, at six in the morning, with a lively
breeze, the river very blue and broken into
ripples, and a lot of little white clouds in the
sky. The air was full of gaiety and sunshine
and the sense of the singing of birds, though
actually, I think, there were only a few gulls
crying. It was the perfection of a summer
morning, thrilling with a freshness which, the

fancy said, was keener than any the old world knew. And high and grey and serene above the morning lay the citadel of Quebec.

Is there any city in the world that stands so nobly as Quebec ? The citadel crowns a headland, three hundred feet high, that juts boldly out into the St Lawrence. Up to it, up the side of the hill, clambers the city, houses and steeples and huts, piled one on the other. It has the individuality and the pride of a city where great things have happened, and over which many years have passed. Quebec is as refreshing and as definite after the other cities of this continent as an immortal among a crowd of stockbrokers. She has, indeed, the radiance and repose of an immortal ; but she wears her immortality youthfully. When you get among the streets of Quebec, the mediæval, precipitous, narrow, winding, and perplexed streets, you begin to realise her charm. She almost incurs the charge of quaintness (abhorrent quality !) ; but even quaintness becomes attractive in this country. You are in a foreign land, for the people have an alien tongue, short stature, the quick, decided, cinematographic quality of movement, and the inexplicable cheerfulness, which mark a foreigner. You might almost be in

Siena or some old German town, except that
Quebec has her street-cars and grain-elevators
to show that she is living.

The American Jew and I took a *calèche*, a
little two-wheeled local carriage, driven by a
lively Frenchman with a factitious passion
for death-spots and churches. A small black
and white spaniel followed the *calèche*, yapping.
The American's face shone with interest.
" That dawg's Michael," he said, " the hotel
dawg. He's a queer little dawg. I kicked his
face ; and he tried to bite me. Hup, Michael ! "
And he laughed hoarsely. " Non ! " said
the driver suddenly, " it is not the 'otel
dog." The American did not lose interest.
" These little dawgs are all alike," he said.
" Dare say if you kicked that dawg in
the face, he'd bite you. Hup, Michael ! "
With that he fell into deep thought.

We rattled up and down the steep streets,
out among tidy fields, and back into the
noisily sedate city again. We saw where
Wolfe fell, where Montcalm fell, where Mont-
gomery fell. Children played where the tides
of war had ebbed and flowed. Mr Norman
Angell and his friends tell us that trade is
superseding war ; and pacifists declare that
for the future countries will win their pride

or shame from commercial treaties and tariffs and bounties, and no more from battles and sieges. And there is a part of Canadian patriotism that has progressed this way. But I wonder if the hearts of that remarkable race, posterity, will ever beat the harder when they are told, " Here Mr Borden stood when he decided to double the duty on agricultural implements," or even " In this room Mr Ritchie conceived the plan of removing the shilling on wheat." When that happens, Quebec will be a forgotten ruin. . . . The reverie was broken by my friend struggling to his feet and standing, unsteady and bareheaded, in the swaying carriage. In that position he burst hoarsely into a song that I recognised as ' The Star-Spangled Banner.' We were passing the American Consulate. His song over, he settled down and fell into a deep sleep, and the *calèche* jolted down even narrower streets, curiously paved with planks, and ways that led through and under the ancient, tottering wooden houses.

But Quebec is too real a city to be ' seen ' in such a manner. And a better way of spending a few days, or years, is to sit on Dufferin Terrace, with the old Lower Town sheer beneath you, and the river beyond it, and the citadel to the right, a little above, and the Isle of Orleans and the French villages away down-stream to your left. Hour by hour the colours change, and sunlight follows shadow, and mist rises, and smoke drifts across. And through the veil of the shifting of lights and hues there remains visible the majesty of the most glorious river in the world.

From this contemplation, and from musing on men's agreement to mark by this one great sign of the Taking of the Heights of Quebec, the turning of one of the greatest currents in our history, I was torn by a journey I had been advised to make. The boat goes some hundred and thirty miles down the St Lawrence, turns up a northern tributary, the Saguenay, goes as far as Chicoutimi, ninety miles up, and returns to Quebec. Both on this trip, and between Quebec and Montreal, we touched at many little French villages, by day and by night. Their *habitants*, the French-Canadian peasants, are a jolly sight. They are like children in their noisy content. They are poor and happy, Roman Catholics; they laugh a great deal ; and they continually sing. They do not progress at all. As a counter to these admirable people we had on our boat a great many priests. They diffused an atmosphere

of black, of unpleasant melancholy. Their
faces had that curiously unwashed look, and
were for the most part of a mean and very
untrustworthy expression. Their eyes were
small, shifty, and cruel, and would not meet
the gaze. . . . The choice between our own
age and mediæval times is a very hard one.

It was almost full night when we left the
twenty-mile width of the St Lawrence, and
turned up a gloomy inlet. By reason of the
night and of comparison with the river from
which we had come, this stream appeared unnaturally narrow. Darkness hid all detail,
and we were only aware of vast cliffs, sometimes dense with trees, sometimes bare faces
of sullen rock. They shut us in, oppressively,
but without heat. There are no banks to this
river, for the most part; only these walls,
rising sheer from the water to the height of
two thousand feet, going down sheer beneath
it, or rather by the side of it, to many times
that depth. The water was of some colour
blacker than black. Even by daylight it is
inky and sinister. It flows without foam or
ripple. No white showed in the wake of the
boat. The ominous shores were without sign
of life, save for a rare light every few miles,
to mark some bend in the chasm. Once a

canoe with two Indians shot out of the shadows, passed under our stern, and vanished silently down stream. We all became hushed and apprehensive. The night was gigantic and terrible. There were a few stars, but the flood slid along too swiftly to reflect them. The whole scene seemed some Stygian imagination of Dante. As we drew further and further into that lightless land, little twists and curls of vapour wriggled over the black river-surface. Our homeless, irrelevant, tiny steamer seemed to hang between two abysms. One became suddenly aware of the miles of dark water beneath. I found that under a prolonged gaze the face of the river began to writhe and eddy, as if from some horrible suppressed emotion. It seemed likely that something might appear. I reflected that if the river failed us, all hope was gone; and that anyhow this region was the abode of devils. I went to bed.

Next day we steamed down the river again. By daylight some of the horror goes, but the impression of ancientness and desolation remains. The gloomy flood is entirely shut in by the rock or the tangled pine and birch forests of these great cliffs, except in one or two places, where a chine and a beach have given lodging to lonely villages. One of these is at the end of a long bay, called Ha-Ha Bay. The local guide-book, an early example of the school of fantastic realism so popular among our younger novelists, says that this name arose from the ' laughing ejaculations ' of the early French explorers, who had mistaken this lengthy blind-alley for the main stream. ' Ha ! Ha ! ' they said. So like an early explorer.

At the point where the Saguenay joins the St Lawrence, here twenty miles wide, I ' stopped off ' for a day, to feel the country more deeply. The village is called Tadousac, and consists of an hotel and French fishermen, to whom Quebec is a distant, unvisited city of legend. The afternoon was very hot. I wandered out along a thin margin of yellow sand to the extreme rocky point where the waters of the two rivers meet and swirl. There I lay, and looked at the strange humps of the Laurentian hills, and the dark green masses of the woods, impenetrable depths of straight and leaning and horizontal trees, broken here and there by great bald granite rocks, and behind me the little village, where the earliest church in Canada stands. Away in the St Lawrence there would be a flash as an immense white fish jumped. Miles out an occasional steamer passed, bound to England perhaps. And once, hugging the coast, came a half-breed paddling a canoe with a small diamond-shaped sail, filled with trout. The cliff above me was crowned with beds of blue flowers, whose names I did not know. Against the little gulfs and coasts of rock at my feet were washing a few white logs of driftwood. I wondered if they could have floated across from England, or if they could be from the *Titanic*. The sun was very hot, the sky a clear light blue, almost cloudless, like an English sky, and the water seemed fairly deep. I stripped, hovered a while on the brink, and plunged. The current was unexpectedly strong. I seemed to feel that two-mile-deep body of black water moving against me. And it was cold as death. Stray shreds of the St Lawrence water were warm and cheerful. But the current of the Saguenay, on such a day, seemed unnaturally icy. As my head came up I made one dash for the land, scrambled out on the hot rocks, and lay there panting. Then I dried on a handkerchief, dressed, and ran back home, still shivering, through the woods to the hotel.

VII
ONTARIO

VII

ONTARIO

THE great joy of travelling in Canada is to do it by water. The advantage of this is that you can keep fairly clean and quiet of nerves; the disadvantage is that you don't 'see the country.' I travelled most of the way from Ottawa to Toronto by water. But between Ottawa and Prescott then, and later from Toronto to Niagara Falls, and thence to Sarnia, there is a good deal of Southern Ontario to be seen—the part which has counted as Ontario so far. And I saw it through a faint grey-pink mist of *Heimweh*. For after the States and after Quebec it is English. There are weather-beaten farm-houses, rolling country, thickets of trees, little hills green and grey in the distance, decorous small fields, orchards, and, I swear, a hedge or two. Most of the towns we went through are a little too vivacious or too pert to be European. But there seemed to be real villages occasionally, and the land had a quiet air of occupation.

Men have lived contentedly on this land and died where they were born, and so given it a certain sanctity. Away north the wild begins, and is only now being brought into civilisation, inhabited, made productive, explored, and exploited. But this country has seen the generations pass, and won something of that repose and security which countries acquire from the sight.

The wise traveller from Ottawa to Toronto catches a boat at Prescott, and puffs judicially between two nations up the St Lawrence and across Lake Ontario. We were a cosmopolitan, middle-class bunch (it is the one distinction between the Canadian and American languages that Canadians tend to say ' bunch ' but Americans ' crowd '), out to enjoy the scenery. For this stretch of the river is notoriously picturesque, containing the Thousand Isles. The Thousand Isles vary from six inches to hundreds of yards in diameter. Each, if big enough, has been bought by a rich man— generally an American—who has built a castle on it. So the whole isn't much more beautiful than Golder's Green. We picked our way carefully between the islands. The Americans on board sat in rows saying " That house was built by Mr ——. Made his money in biscuits.

Cost three hundred thousand dollars, e-recting that building. Yessir." The Canadians sat looking out the other way, and said, " In nineteen-ten this land was worth twenty thousand an acre; now it's worth forty-five thousand. Next year . . . . " and their eyes grew solemn as the eyes of men who think deep and holy thoughts. But the English sat quite still, looking straight in front of them, thinking of nothing at all, and hoping that nobody would speak to them. So we fared; until, well on in the afternoon, we came to the entrance of Lake Ontario.

There is something ominous and unnatural about these great lakes. The sweet flow of a river, and the unfriendly restless vitality of the sea, men may know and love. And the little lakes we have in Europe are but as fresh-water streams that have married and settled down, alive and healthy and comprehensible. Rivers (except the Saguenay) are human. The sea, very properly, will not be allowed in heaven. It has no soul. It is unvintageable, cruel, treacherous, what you will. But, in the end—while we have it with us—it is all right; even though that all-rightness result but, as with France, from the recognition of an age-long feud and an irremediable lack of sympathy. But these monstrous lakes, which ape the ocean, are not proper to fresh water or salt. They have souls, perceptibly, and wicked ones.

We steamed out, that day, over a flat, stationary mass of water, smooth with the smoothness of metal or polished stone or one's finger-nail. There was a slight haze everywhere. The lake was a terrible dead-silver colour, the gleam of its surface shot with flecks of blue and a vapoury enamel-green. It was like a gigantic silver shield. Its glint was inexplicably sinister and dead, like the glint on glasses worn by a blind man. In front the steely mist hid the horizon, so that the occasional rock or little island and the one ship in sight seemed hung in air. They were reflected to a preternatural length in the glassy floor. Our boat appeared to leave no wake; those strange waters closed up foamlessly behind her. But our black smoke hung, away back on the trail, in a thick, clearly-bounded cloud, becalmed in the hot, windless air, very close over the water, like an evil soul after death that cannot win dissolution. Behind us and to the right lay the low, woody shores of Southern Ontario and Prince Edward Peninsula, long dark lines of green, stretching thinner and thinner, interminably, into the distance. The lake around us was dull, though the sun shone full on it. It gleamed, but without radiance.

Toronto (pronounce *T'ranto*, please) is difficult to describe. It has an individuality, but an elusive one; yet not through any queerness or difficult shade of eccentricity; a subtly normal, an indefinably obvious personality. It is a healthy, cheerful city (by modern standards); a clean-shaven, pink-faced, respectably dressed, fairly energetic, unintellectual, passably sociable, well-to-do, public-school-and-'varsity sort of city. One knows in one's own life certain bright and pleasant figures; people who occupy the nearer middle distance, unobtrusive but not negligible; wardens of the marches between acquaintance-ship and friendship. It is always nice to meet them, and in parting one looks back at them once. They are, healthily and simply, the most fitting product of a not perfect environment; good-sorts; normal, but not too normal; distinctly themselves, but not distinguished. They support civilisation. You can trust them in anything, if your demand be for nothing extremely intelligent or absurdly altruistic. One of these could be exhibited

in any gallery in the universe, ' Perfect Specimen ; Upper Middle Classes ; Twentieth
Century '—and we should not be ashamed.
They are not vexed by impossible dreams,
nor outrageously materialistic, nor perplexed
by overmuch prosperity, nor spoilt by reverse. Souls for whom the wind is always
nor'-nor'-west, and they sail nearer success
than failure, and nearer wisdom than lunacy.
Neither leaders nor slaves—but no Tomlinsons !
—whomsoever of your friends you miss, *them*
you will certainly meet again, not unduly
pardoned, the fifty-first by the Throne.

Such is Toronto. A brisk city of getting
on for half a million inhabitants, the largest
British city in Canada (in spite of the cheery
Italian faces that pop up at you out of excava-
tions in the street), liberally endowed with
millionaires, not lacking its due share of destitution, misery, and slums. It is no mushroom
city of the West, it has its history ; but at
the same time it has grown immensely of recent
years. It is situated on the shores of a lovely
lake ; but you never see that, because the
railways have occupied the entire lake front.
So if, at evening, you try to find your way to
the edge of the water, you are checked by a
region of smoke, sheds, trucks, wharves, store-

houses, 'depôts,' railway-lines, signals, and locomotives and trains that wander on the tracks up and down and across streets, pushing their way through the pedestrians, and tolling, as they go, in the American fashion, an immense melancholy bell, intent, apparently, on some private and incommunicable grief. Higher up are the business quarters, a few sky-scrapers in the American style without the modern American beauty, but one of which advertises itself as the highest in the British Empire ; streets that seem less narrow than Montreal, but not unrespectably wide ; " the buildings are generally substantial and often handsome " (the too kindly Herr Baedeker). Beyond that the residential part, with quiet streets, gardens open to the road, shady verandahs, and homes, generally of wood, that are a deal more pleasant to see than the houses in a modern English town.

Toronto is the centre and heart of the Province of Ontario ; and Ontario, with a third of the whole population of Canada, directs the country for the present, conditioned by the French on one hand and the West on the other. And in this land, that is as yet hardly at all conscious of itself as a nation, Toronto and Ontario do their best in leading and realising national sentiment. A Toronto man, like most Canadians, dislikes an Englishman; but, unlike some Canadians, he detests an American. And he has some inkling of the conditions and responsibilities of the British Empire. The tradition is in him. His fathers fought to keep Canada British.

It is never easy to pick out of the turmoil of an election the real powers that have moved men; and it is especially difficult in a country where politics are so corrupt as they are in Canada. But certainly this British feeling helped to throw Ontario, and so the country, against Reciprocity with the United States in 1911; and it is keeping it, in the comedy of the Navy Question, on Mr Borden's side— rather from distrust of his opponents' sincerity, perhaps, than from admiration of the fix he is in. It has been used, this patriotism, to aid the wealthy interests, which are all-power-ful here; and it will continue to be a ball in the tennis of party politics. But it is real; it will remain, potential of good, among all the forces that are certain for evil.

Toronto, soul of Canada, is wealthy, busy, commercial, Scotch, absorbent of whisky; but she is duly aware of other things. She has a most modern and efficient interest in education; and here are gathered what faint, faint beginnings or premonitions of such things as Art Canada can boast (except the French-Canadians, who, it is complained, produce disproportionately much literature, and waste their time on their own unprofitable songs). Most of those few who have begun to paint the landscape of Canada centre there, and a handful of people who know about books. In these things, as in all, this city is properly and cheerfully to the front. It can scarcely be doubted that the first Repertory Theatre in Canada will be founded in Toronto, some thirty years hence, and will very daringly perform *Candida* and *The Silver Box*. Canada is a live country, live, but not, like the States, kicking. In these trifles of Art and ' culture,' indeed, she is much handicapped by the proximity of the States. For her poets and writers are apt to be drawn thither, for the better companionship there and the higher rates of pay.

But Toronto—Toronto is the subject. One must say something—*what* must one say about Toronto ? What can one ? What has anybody ever said ? It is impossible to give it anything but commendation. It is not squalid like Birmingham, or cramped like Canton,

or scattered like Edmonton, or sham like
Berlin, or hellish like New York, or tiresome
like Nice.   It is all right.   The only depressing
thing is that it will always be what it is, only
larger, and that no Canadian city can ever be
anything better or different.   If they are good
they may become Toronto.

VIII

NIAGARA FALLS

VIII

NIAGARA FALLS

SAMUEL BUTLER has a lot to answer for. But for him, a modern traveller could spend his time peacefully admiring the scenery instead of feeling himself bound to dog the simple and grotesque of the world for the sake of their too-human comments. It is his fault if a peasant's *naïveté* has come to outweigh the beauty of rivers, and the remarks of clergymen are more than mountains. It is very restful to give up all effort at observing human nature and drawing social and political deductions from trifles, and to let oneself relapse into wide-mouthed worship of the wonders of nature. And this is very easy at Niagara. Niagara means nothing. It is not leading anywhere. It does not result from anything. It throws no light on the effects of Protection, nor on the Facility for Divorce in America, nor on Corruption in Public Life, nor on Canadian character, nor even on the Navy Bill. It is merely a great deal of water falling

over some cliffs. But it is very remarkably
that. The human race, apt as a child to
destroy what it admires, has done its best
to surround the Falls with every distraction,
incongruity, and vulgarity. Hotels, power-
houses, bridges, trams, picture post-cards,
sham legends, stalls, booths, rifle-galleries,
and side-shows frame them about. And
there are Touts. Niagara is the central home
and breeding-place for all the touts of earth.
There are touts insinuating, and touts raucous,
greasy touts, brazen touts, and upper-class,
refined, gentlemanly, take-you-by-the-arm
touts; touts who intimidate and touts who
wheedle; professionals, amateurs, and *dilet-
tanti*, male and female; touts who would
photograph you with your arm round a
young lady against a faked background of
the sublimest cataract, touts who would
bully you into cars, char-à-bancs, elevators, or
tunnels, or deceive you into a carriage and
pair, touts who would sell you picture post-
cards, moccasins, sham Indian beadwork,
blankets, tee-pees, and crockery; and touts,
finally, who have no apparent object in the
world, but just purely, simply, merely, incessantly, indefatigably, and ineffugibly—to
tout. And in the midst of all this, over-

whelming it all, are the Falls. He who sees them instantly forgets humanity. They are not very high, but they are overpowering. They are divided by an island into two parts, the Canadian and the American.

Half a mile or so above the Falls, on either side, the water of the great stream begins to run more swiftly and in confusion. It descends with ever-growing speed. It begins chattering and leaping, breaking into a thousand ripples, throwing up joyful fingers of spray. Sometimes it is divided by islands and rocks. sometimes the eye can see nothing but a waste of laughing, springing, foamy waves, turning, crossing, even seeming to stand for an instant erect, but always borne impetuously forward like a crowd of triumphant feasters. Sit close down by it, and you see a fragment of the torrent against the sky, mottled, steely, and foaming, leaping onward in far-flung criss-cross strands of water. Perpetually the eye is on the point of descrying a pattern in this weaving, and perpetually it is cheated by change. In one place part of the flood plunges over a ledge a few feet high and a quarter of a mile or so long, in a uniform and stable curve. It gives an impression of almost military con-

certed movement, grown suddenly out of
confusion. But it is swiftly lost again in the
multitudinous tossing merriment. Here and
there a rock close to the surface is marked
by a white wave that faces backwards and
seems to be rushing madly up-stream, but
is really stationary in the headlong charge.
But for these signs of reluctance, the waters
seem to fling themselves on with some fore-
knowledge of their fate, in an ever wilder
frenzy. But it is no Maeterlinckian pre-
science. They prove, rather, that Greek
belief that the great crashes are preceded
by a louder merriment and a wilder gaiety.
Leaping in the sunlight, careless, entwining,
clamorously joyful, the waves riot on towards the verge.

But there they change. As they turn to
the sheer descent, the white and blue and
slate-colour, in the heart of the Canadian
Falls at least, blend and deepen to a rich,
wonderful, luminous green. On the edge
of disaster the river seems to gather herself,
to pause, to lift a head noble in ruin, and
then, with a slow grandeur, to plunge into
the eternal thunder and white chaos below.
Where the stream runs shallower it is a kind
of violet colour, but both violet and green

fray and frill to white as they fall. The mass of water, striking some ever-hidden base of rock, leaps up the whole two hundred feet again in pinnacles and domes of spray. The spray falls back into the lower river once more; all but a little that fines to foam and white mist, which drifts in layers along the air, graining it, and wanders out on the wind over the trees and gardens and houses, and so vanishes.

The manager of one of the great power-stations on the banks of the river above the Falls told me that the centre of the river-bed at the Canadian Falls is deep and of a saucer shape. So it may be possible to fill this up to a uniform depth, and divert a lot of water for the power-houses. And this, he said, would supply the need for more power, which will certainly soon arise, without taking away from the beauty of Niagara. This is a handsome concession of the utilitarians to ordinary sight-seers. Yet, I doubt if we shall be satisfied. The real secret of the beauty and terror of the Falls is not their height or width, but the feeling of colossal power and of unintelligible disaster caused by the plunge of that vast body of water. If that were taken away, there would be little visible change; but the heart would be gone.

The American Falls do not inspire this feeling in the same way as the Canadian. It is because they are less in volume, and because the water does not fall so much into one place. By comparison their beauty is almost delicate and fragile. They are extraordinarily level, one long curtain of lacework and woven foam. Seen from opposite, when the sun is on them, they are blindingly white, and the clouds of spray show dark against them. With both Falls the colour of the water is the ever-altering wonder. Greens and blues, purples and whites, melt into one another, fade, and come again, and change with the changing sun. Sometimes they are as richly diaphanous as a precious stone, and glow from within with a deep, inexplicable light. Sometimes the white intricacies of dropping foam become opaque and creamy. And always there are the rainbows. If you come suddenly upon the Falls from above, a great double rainbow, very vivid, spanning the extent of spray from top to bottom, is the first thing you see. If you wander along the cliff opposite, a bow springs into being in the American Falls, accompanies you courteously on your walk, dwindles and dies as the mist ends, and awakens again as you reach the Canadian tumult. And the bold traveller who attempts the trip under the American Falls sees, when he dare open his eyes to anything, tiny baby rainbows, some four or five yards in span, leaping from rock to rock among the foam, and gambolling beside him, barely out of hand's reach, as he goes. One I saw in that place was a complete circle, such as I have never seen before, and so near that I could put my foot on it. It is a terrifying journey, beneath and behind the Falls. The senses are battered and bewildered by the thunder of the water and the assault of wind and spray; or rather, the sound is not of falling water, but merely of falling; a noise of unspecified ruin. So, if you are close behind the endless clamour, the sight cannot recognise liquid in the masses that hurl past. You are dimly and pitifully aware that sheets of light and darkness are falling in great curves in front of you. Dull omnipresent foam washes the face. Farther away, in the roar and hissing, clouds of spray seem literally to slide down some invisible plane of air.

Beyond the foot of the Falls the river is

like a slipping floor of marble, green with
veins of dirty white, made by the scum that
was foam. It slides very quietly and slowly
down for a mile or two, sullenly exhausted.
Then it turns to a dull sage green, and hurries
more swiftly, smooth and ominous. As the
walls of the ravine close in, trouble stirs, and
the waters boil and eddy. These are the
lower rapids, a sight more terrifying than the
Falls, because less intelligible. Close in its
bands of rock the river surges tumultuously
forward, writhing and leaping as if inspired
by a demon. It is pressed by the straits
into a visibly convex form. Great planes
of water slide past. Sometimes it is thrown
up into a pinnacle of foam higher than
a house, or leaps with incredible speed
from the crest of one vast wave to another,
along the shining curve between, like the
spring of a wild beast. Its motion continually suggests muscular action. The power
manifest in these rapids moves one with a
different sense of awe and terror from that
of the Falls. Here the inhuman life and
strength are spontaneous, active, almost re-
solute; masculine vigour compared with the
passive gigantic power, female, helpless and
overwhelming, of the Falls. A place of fear.

One is drawn back, strangely, to a contemplation of the Falls, at every hour, and especially by night, when the cloud of spray becomes an immense visible ghost, straining and wavering high above the river, white and pathetic and translucent. The Victorian lies very close below the surface in every man. There one can sit and let great cloudy thoughts of destiny and the passage of empires drift through the mind ; for such dreams are at home by Niagara. I could not get out of my mind the thought of a friend, who said that the rainbows over the Falls were like the arts and beauty and goodness, with regard to the stream of life—caused by it, thrown upon its spray, but unable to stay or direct or affect it, and ceasing when it ceased. In all comparisons that rise in the heart, the river, with its multitudinous waves and its single current, likens itself to a life, whether of an individual or of a community. A man's life is of many flashing moments, and yet one stream ; a nation's flows through all its citizens, and yet is more than they. In such places, one is aware, with an almost insupportable and yet comforting certitude, that both men and nations are hurried onwards to their ruin or ending as inevitably as this dark flood.   Some go down to it unreluctant, and meet it, like the river, not without nobility.   And as incessant, as inevitable, and as unavailing as the spray that hangs over the Falls, is the white cloud of human crying. . . . With some such thoughts does the platitudinous heart win from the confusion and thunder of Niagara a peace that the quietest plains or most stable hills can never give.

IX

TO WINNIPEG

IX

TO WINNIPEG

THE boats that run from Sarnia the whole length of Lake Huron and Lake Superior are not comfortable. But no doubt a train for those six hundred miles would be worse. You start one afternoon, and in the morning of the next day you have done with the rather colourless, unindividual expanses of Huron, and are dawdling along a canal that joins the lakes by the little town of Sault Ste. Marie (pronounced, abruptly, ' Soo '). We happened on it one Sunday. The nearer waters of the river and the lakes were covered with little sailing or rowing or bathing parties. Everybody seemed cheerful, merry, and mildly raucous. There is a fine, breezy, enviable healthiness about Canadian life. Except in some Eastern cities, there are few clerks or working-men but can get away to the woods and water.

As we drew out into the cold magnificence of Lake Superior, the receding woody shores were occasionally spotted with picnickers or campers, who rushed down the beach in various deshabille, waving towels, handkerchiefs, or garments. We were as friendly. The human race seemed a jolly bunch, and the world a fine, pleasant, open-air affair—'some world,' in fact. A man in a red shirt and a bronzed girl with flowing hair slid past in a canoe. We whistled, sang, and cried 'Snooky-ookums!' and other words of occult meaning, which imputed love to them, and foolishness. They replied suitably, grinned, and were gone. A little old lady in black, in the chair next mine, kept a small telescope glued to her eye, hour after hour. Whenever she distinguished life on any shore we passed, she waved a tiny handkerchief. Diligently she did this, and with grave face, never visible to the objects of her devotion, I suppose, but certainly very happy ; the most persistent lover of humanity I have ever seen. . . .

In the afternoon we were beyond sight of land. The world grew a little chilly ; and over the opaque, hueless water came sliding a queer, pale mist. We strained through it for hours, a low bank of cloud, not twenty feet in height, on which one could look down from the higher deck. Its upper surface was quite flat and smooth, save for innumerable tiny molehills or pyramids of mist. We seemed to be ploughing aimlessly through the phantasmal sand-dunes of another world, faintly and by an accident apprehended. So may the shades on a ghostly liner, plunging down Lethe, have an hour's chance glimpse of the lights and lives of Piccadilly, to them uncertain and filmy mirages of the air.

To taste the full deliciousness of travelling in an American train by night through new scenery, you must carefully secure a lower berth. And when you are secret and separate in your little oblong world, safe between sheets, pull up the blinds on the great window a few inches and leave them so. Thus, as you lie, you can view the dark procession of woods and hills, and mingle the broken hours of railway slumber with glimpses of 'a wild starlit landscape. The country retains individuality, and yet puts on romance, especially the rough, shaggy region between Port Arthur and Winnipeg. For four hundred miles there is hardly a sign that humanity exists on the earth's face, only rocks and endless woods of scrubby pine, and the occasional strange gleam of water, and night and the wind. Night-long, dream and reality mingle. You may wake from sleep to find yourself flying through a region where a forest fire has passed, a place of grey pine-trunks, stripped of foliage, occasionally waving a naked bough. They appear stricken by calamity, intolerably bare and lonely, gaunt, perpetually protesting, amazed and tragic creatures. We saw no actual fire the night I passed. But a little while after dawn we noticed on the horizon, fifteen miles away, an immense column of smoke. There was little wind, and it hung, as if sculptured, against the grey of the morning; nor did we lose sight of it till just before we boomed over a wide, swift, muddy river, into the flat city of Winnipeg.

Winnipeg is the West. It is important and obvious that in Canada there are two or three (some say five) distinct Canadas. Even if you lump the French and English together as one community in the East, there remains the gulf of the Great Lakes. The difference between East and West is possibly no greater than that between North and South England, or Bavaria and Prussia; but in this country, yet unconscious of itself, there is so much less to hold them together. The character of the land and the people differs; their interests,

as it appears to them, are not the same.
Winnipeg is a new city. In the archives at
Ottawa is a picture of Winnipeg in 1870—
Mainstreet, with a few shacks, and the prairie
either end. Now her population is a hundred
thousand, and she has the biggest this, that,
and the other west of Toronto. A new city ; a
little more American than the other Canadian
cities, but not unpleasantly so. The streets
are wider, and full of a bustle which keeps
clear of hustle. The people have something
of the free swing of Americans, without the
bumptiousness ; a tempered democracy, a
mitigated independence of bearing. The
manners of Winnipeg, of the West, impress
the stranger as better than those of the East,
more friendly, more hearty, more certain to
achieve graciousness, if not grace. There is,
even, in the architecture of Winnipeg, a sort
of *gauche* pride visible. It is hideous, of
course, even more hideous than Toronto or
Montreal ; but cheerily and windily so. There
is no scheme in the city, and no beauty, but
it is at least preferable to Birmingham, less
dingy, less directly depressing. It has no
real slums, even though there is poverty and
destitution.

But there seems to be a trifle more public

spirit in the West than the East.   Perhaps it is that in the greater eagerness and confidence of this newer country men have a superfluity of energy and interest, even after attending to their own affairs, to give to the community. Perhaps it is that the West is so young that one has a suspicion money-making has still some element of a child's game in it—its only excuse.   At any rate, whether because the state of affairs is yet unsettled, or because of the invisible subtle spirit of optimism that blows through the heavily clustering telephone-wires and past the neat little modern villas and down the solidly pretentious streets, one can't help finding a tiny hope that Winnipeg, the city of buildings and the city of human beings, may yet come to something.   It is a slender hope, not to be compared to that of the true Winnipeg man, who, gazing on his city, is fired with the proud and secret ambition that it will soon be twice as big, and after that four times, and then ten times . . .

> "Wider still and wider
> Shall thy bounds be set,"

says that hymn which is the noblest expression of modern ambition.   *That* hope is sure to be fulfilled.   But the other timid prayer, that something different, something more worth having, may come out of Winnipeg, exists, and not quite unreasonably. That cannot be said of Toronto.

Winnipeg is of the West, new, vigorous in its way, of unknown potentialities. Already the West has been a nuisance to the East, in the fight of 1911 over Reciprocity with the United States. When she gets a larger representation in Parliament, she will be still more of a nuisance. A casual traveller cannot venture to investigate the beliefs and opinions of the inhabitants of a country, but he can record them all the better, perhaps, for his foreign-ness. It is generally believed in the West that the East runs Canada, and runs it for its own advantage. And the East means a very few rich men, who control the big railways, the banks, and the Manufacturers' Association, subscribe to both political parties, and are generally credited with complete control over the Tariff and most other Canadian affairs. Whether or no the Manufacturers' Association does arrange the Tariff and control the commerce of Canada, it is generally believed to do so. The only thing is that its friends say that it acts in the best interests of Canada, its enemies that it acts in the best interests of the Manufacturers' Association. Among its enemies are many in the West. The normal Western life is a lonely and individual one ; and a large part of the population has crossed from the United States, or belongs to that great mass of European immigration that Canada is letting so blindly in. So, naturally, the Westerner does not feel the same affection for the Empire or for England as the British Canadians of the East, whose forefathers fought to stay within the Empire. Nor is his affection increased by the suspicion that the Imperial cry has been used for party purposes. He has no use for politics at Ottawa. The naval question is nothing to him. He wants neither to subscribe money nor to build ships. Europe is very far away ; and he is too ignorant to realise his close connection with her. He has strong views, however, on a Tariff which only affects him by perpetually raising the cost of living and farming. The ideas of even a Conservative in the West about reducing the Tariff would make an Eastern ' Liberal ' die of heart-failure. And the Westerner also hates the Banks. The banking system of Canada is peculiar, and throws the control of the banks into the hands of a few people in the East, who were felt, by the ever optimistic West, to have shut down credit too completely during the recent money stringency.

The most interesting expression of the new Western point of view, and in many ways the most hopeful movement in Canada, is the Co-operative movement among the grain-growers of the three prairie provinces. Only started a few years ago, it has grown rapidly in numbers, wealth, power, and extent of operations. So far it has confined itself politically to influencing provincial legislatures. But it has gradually attached itself to an advanced Radical programme of a Chartist description. And it is becoming powerful. Whether the outcome will be a very desirable rejuvenation of the Liberal Party, or the creation of a third—perhaps Radical-Labour—party, it is hard to tell. At any rate, the change will come. And, just to start with, there will very shortly come to the Eastern Powers, who threw out Reciprocity with the States for the sake of the Empire, a demand from the West that the preference to British goods be increased rapidly till they be allowed to come in free, also for the Empire's sake. Then the fun will begin.

X
OUTSIDE

X

OUTSIDE

I HAD visited New York, Boston, Quebec,
Montreal, and Toronto. In Winnipeg I
found a friend, who was tired of cities. So
was I. In Canada the remedy lies close at
hand. We took ancient clothes—and I, Ben
Jonson and Jane Austen to keep me English
—and departed northward for a lodge, re-
ported to exist in a region of lakes and hills
and forests and caribou and Indians and a few
people. At first the train sauntered through
a smiling plain, intermittently cultivated, and
dotted with little new villages. Over this
country are thrown little pools of that flood
of European immigration that pours through
Winnipeg, to remain separate or be absorbed,
as destiny wills. The problem of immigration
here reveals that purposelessness that exists
in the affairs of Canada even more than those
of other nations. The multitude from South
or East Europe flocks in. Some make money
and return. The most remain, often in in-

assimilable lumps. There is every sign that these lumps may poison the health of Canada as dangerously as they have that of the United States. For Canada there is the peril of too large an element of foreign blood and traditions in a small nation already little more than half composed of British blood and descent. Nationalities seem to teach one another only their worst. If the Italians gave the Canadians of their good manners, and the Doukhobors or Poles inoculated them with idealism and the love of beauty, and received from them British romanticism and sense of responsibility ! . . . . But they only seem to increase the anarchy, these ' foreigners,' and to learn the American twang and method of spitting. And there is the peril of politics. Upon these scattered exotic communities, ignorant of the problems of their adopted land, ignorant even of its language, swoop the agents of political parties, with their one effectual argument—bad whisky. This baptism is the immigrants' only organised welcome into their new liberties. Occasionally some Church raises a thin protest. But the ' Anglo-Saxon ' continues to take up his burden ; and the floods from Europe pour in. Canadians regard this influx with that queer fatalism which men adopt under plutocracy. "How could they stop it? It pays the steamship and railway companies. It may, or may not, be good for Canada. Who knows? In any case, it will go on. Our masters wish it. . . ."

It is noteworthy that Icelanders are found to be far the readiest to mingle and become Canadian. After them, Norwegians and Swedes. With other immigrant nationalities, hope lies with the younger generation; but these acclimatise immediately.

Our train was boarded by a crowd of Ruthenians or Galicians, brown-eyed and beautiful people, not yet wholly civilised out of their own costume. The girls chatted together in a swift, lovely language, and the children danced about, tossing their queer brown mops of hair. They clattered out at a little village that seemed to belong to them, and stood waving and laughing us out of sight. I pondered on their feelings, and looked for the name of the little Utopia these aliens had found in a new world. It was called (for the railway companies name towns in this country) ' Milner.'

We wandered into rougher country, where the rocks begin to show through the surface, and scrub pine abounds. At the end of our side-line was another, and at the end of that a village, the ultimate outpost of civilisation. Here, on the way back, some weeks later, we had to spend the night in a little hotel which ' accommodated transients.' It was a rough affair of planks, inhabited by whatever wandering workman from construction-camps or other labour in the region wanted shelter for the night.   You slept in a sort of dormitory, each bed partitioned off from the rest by walls that were some feet short of the ceiling. Swedes, Germans, Welsh, Italians, and Poles occupied the other partitions, each blaspheming the works of the Lord in his own tongue. About midnight two pairs of feet crashed into the cell opposite mine ; and a high, sleepless voice, with an accent I knew, continued an interminable argument on theology.   " I' beginning wash word," it proclaimed with all the melancholy of drunkenness. The other disputant was German or Norwegian, and uninterested, though very kindly. " Right-o ! " he said. " Let's go sleep ! "

" *What* word ? " pondered the Englishman. The Norwegian suggested several, sleepily. " Logos," wailed the other, " *What* Logos ? " and wept. They persisted, hour by hour,

disconnected voices in the void and darkness,
lonely and chance companions in the back-
blocks of Canada, the one who couldn't, and
the one who didn't want to, understand. A
little before dawn I woke again. That thin
voice, in patient soliloquy, was discussing
Female Suffrage, going very far down into the
roots of the matter. I met its owner next
morning. He was tall and dark and lachry-
mose, with bloodshot eyes, and breath that
stank of gin. He had played scrum-half for
—— College in '98; and had prepared for
ordination. " You'll understand, old man,"
he said, " how out of place I am amongst this
scum—οἱ πολλοί—we're not of the οἱ πολλοί, are
we ? " It seemed nicer to agree. " Oh, I
know Greek ! "—he was too eagerly the gentleman—" ὁ κόσμος τῆς ἀδικίας—the last thing I
learnt for ordination—this world of injustice
—that's right, isn't it ? " He laughed sickly.
" I say as one 'Varsity man to another—we're
not οἱ πολλοί — could you lend me some
money ? "

We had to press on thirty miles up a ' light
railway ' to a power-station, a settlement by
a waterfall in the wild. An engine and an
ancient luggage-van conveyed us. The van
held us, three crates, and some sacks, four

half-breeds in black slouch hats, who curled up on the floor like dogs and slept, and an aged Italian. This last knew no word of English. He had travelled all the way from Naples, Heaven knows how, to find his two sons, supposed to be working in the power-station. So much was written on a piece of paper. We gave him chocolate, and at intervals I repeated to him my only Italian, the first line of the *Divina Commedia*. He seemed cheered. The van jolted on through the fading light. Once a man stepped out on to the track, stopped us, and clambered silently up. We went on. It was the doctor, who had been visiting some lonely hut in the woods. Later, another figure was seen staggering between the rails. We slowed up, shouted, and finally stopped, butting him gently on the back with our buffers, and causing him to fall. He was very drunk. The driver and the doctor helped him into the van. There he stood, and looking round, said very distinctly, " I do not wish to travel on your —— —— train." So we put him off again, and proceeded. Such is the West.

We rattled interminably through the darkness. The unpeopled woods closed about us, snatched with lean branches, and opened out

again to a windy space. Once or twice the
ground fell away, and there was, for a moment,
the mysterious gleam and stir of water.
Canadian stars are remote and virginal.
Everyone slumbered. Arrival at the great
concrete building and the little shacks of the
power-station shook us to our feet. The
Italian vanished into the darkness. Whether
he found his sons or fell into the river no one
knew, and no one seemed to care.

An Indian, taciturn and Mongolian, led us
on next day, by boat and on foot, to the
lonely log-house we aimed at. It stood on
high rocks, above a lake six miles by two.
There was an Indian somewhere, by a river
three miles west, and a trapper to the east,
and a family encamped on an island in the
lake. Else nobody.

It is that feeling of fresh loneliness that
impresses itself before any detail of the wild.
The soul—or the personality—seems to have
indefinite room to expand. There is no one
else within reach, there never has been anyone; no one else is *thinking* of the lakes
and hills you see before you. They have no
tradition, no names even; they are only pools
of water and lumps of earth, some day, perhaps, to be clothed with loves and memories

and the comings and goings of men, but now dumbly waiting their Wordsworth or their Acropolis to give them individuality, and a soul. In such country as this there is a rarefied clean sweetness. The air is unbreathed, and the earth untrodden. All things share this childlike loveliness, the grey whispering reeds, the pure blue of the sky, the birches and thin fir-trees that make up these forests, even the brisk touch of the clear water as you dive.

That last sensation, indeed, and none of sight or hearing, has impressed itself as the token of Canada, the land. Every swimmer knows it. It is not languorous, like bathing in a warm Southern sea ; nor grateful, like a river in a hot climate ; nor strange, as the ocean always is ; nor startling, like very cold water. But it touches the body continually with freshness, and it seems to be charged with a subtle and unexhausted energy. It is colourless, faintly stinging, hard and grey, like the rocks around, full of vitality, and sweet. It has the tint and sensation of a pale dawn before the sun is up. Such is the wild of Canada. It awaits the sun, the end for which Heaven made it, the blessing of civilisation. Some day it will be sold in large portions, and the timber given to a friend of ——'s, and cut down and made into paper, on which shall be printed the praise of prosperity ; and the land itself shall be divided into town-lots and sold, and sub-divided and sold again, and boomed and resold, and boosted and distributed to fishy young men who will vend it in distant parts of the country ; and then such portions as can never be built upon shall be given in exchange for great sums of money to old ladies in the quieter parts of England, but the central parts of towns shall remain in the hands of the wise. And on these shall churches, hotels, and a great many ugly sky-scrapers be built, and hovels for the poor, and houses for the rich, none beautiful, and there shall ugly objects be manufactured, rather hurriedly, and sold to the people at more than they are worth, because similar and cheaper objects made in other countries are kept out by a tariff. . . .

But at present there are only the wrinkled, grey-blue lake, sliding ever sideways, and the grey rocks, and the cliffs and hills, covered with birch-trees, and the fresh wind among the birches, and quiet, and that unseizable virginity. Dawn is always a lost pearly glow in the ashen skies, and sunset a multitude of softly-tinted mists sliding before a remotely golden West.

They follow one another with an infinite loneliness. And there is a far and solitary beach of dark, golden sand, close by a deserted Indian camp, where, if you drift quietly round the corner in a canoe, you may see a bear stumbling along, or a great caribou, or a little red deer coming down to the water to drink, treading the wild edge of lake and forest with a light, secret, and melancholy grace.

XI

THE PRAIRIES

THE PRAIRIES

I PASSED the last few hours of the westward journey from Winnipeg to Regina in daylight, the daylight of a wet and cheerless Sunday. The car was half-empty, in possession of a family of small children and some theatrical ladies and gentlemen from the United States, travelling on ' one night stands,' who were collectively called ' The World-Renowned Barbary Pirates.' We jogged limply from little village to little village, each composed of little brown log-shacks, with a few buildings of tin and corrugated iron, and even of brick, and several grain-elevators. Each village— I beg your pardon, ' town '—seems to be exactly like the next. They differ a little in size, from populations of 100 to nearly 2000, and in age, for some have buildings dating almost back to the nineteenth century, and a few are still mostly tents. They seemed all to be emptied of their folk this Sabbath morn ; though whether the inhabitants were at work, or in church, or had shot themselves from depression induced by the weather, it was impossible to tell. These little towns do not look to the passer-by comfortable as homes. Partly, there is the difficulty of distinguishing your village from the others. It would be as bad as being married to a Jap. And then towns should be on hills or in valleys, however small. A town dumped down, apparently by chance, on a flat expanse, wears the same air of discomfort as a man trying to make his bed on a level, unyielding surface such as a lawn or pavement. He feels hopelessly incidental to the superficies of the earth. He is aware that the human race has thigh-bones. . . .

Yet this country is not quite flat, as I had been led to expect. It does not give you that feeling of a plain you have in parts of Lombardy and Holland and Belgium. This may have been due to the grey mist and drizzle which curtained off the horizon. But the land was always very slightly rolling, and sometimes almost as uneven as a Surrey common. At first it seemed to be given to mixed farming a good deal; afterwards to wheat, oats, and barley. But a great part is uncultivated prairie-land, grass, with sparse bushes and patches of brushwood and a few

rare trees, and continual clumps of large
golden daisies. Occasional rough black roads
wind through the brush and into the towns,
and die into grass tracks along the wire fences.
The day I went through, the interminable,
oblique, thin rain took the gold out of the
wheat and the brown from the distant fields
and bushes, and drabbed all the colours
in the grass. The children in the car cried
to each other with the shrill, sick persist-
ency of tired childhood, " How many inches
to Regina ? " " A Billion." " A Trillion."
" A Shillion." The Barbary Pirates laughed
incessantly. It seemed to me that the
prairie would be a lonely place to live in,
especially if it rained. But the people who
have lived there for years tell me they get
very homesick if they go away for a time.
Valleys and hills seem to them petty, fretful,
unlovable. The magic of the plains has them
in thrall.

Certainly there is a little more democracy
in the west of Canada than the east ; the
communities seem a little less incapable of
looking after themselves. Out in the west
they are erecting not despicable public buildings, founding universities, running a few
public services. That ' politics ' has a voice

in these undertakings does not make them valueless. There are perceptible in the prairies, among all the corruption, irresponsibility, and disastrous individualism, some faint signs of the sense of the community. Take a very good test, the public libraries. As you traverse Canada from east to west they steadily improve. You begin in the city of Montreal, which is unable to support one, and pass through the dingy rooms and inadequate intellectual provision of Toronto and Winnipeg. After that the libraries and reading-rooms, small for the smaller cities, are cleaner and better kept, show signs of care and intelligence ; until at last, in Calgary, you find a very neat and carefully kept building, stocked with an immense variety of periodicals, and an admirably chosen store of books, ranging from the classics to the most utterly modern literature. Few large English towns could show anything as good. Cross the Rockies to Vancouver, and you're back among dirty walls, grubby furniture, and inadequate literature again. There's nothing in Canada to compare with the magnificent libraries little New Zealand can show. But Calgary is hopeful.

These cities grow in population with unimaginable velocity. From thirty to thirty

thousand in fifteen years is the usual rate.
Pavements are laid down, stores and bigger
stores and still bigger stores spring up. Trams
buzz along the streets towards the unregarded
horizon that lies across the end of most roads
in these flat, geometrically planned, prairie-
towns. Probably a Chinese quarter appears,
and the beginnings of slums. Expensive and
pleasant small dwelling-houses fringe the out-
skirts ; and rents being so high, great edifices
of residential flats rival the great stores. In
other streets, or even sandwiched between the
finer buildings, are dingy and decaying saloons,
and innumerable little booths and hovels
where adventurers deal dishonestly in Real
Estate, and Employment Bureaux. And there
are the vast erections of the great corporations,
Hudson's Bay Company, and the banks and
the railways, and, sometimes almost equally
impressive, the public buildings. There are
the beginnings of very costly Universities ;
and Regina has built a superb great House
of Parliament, with a wide sheet of water in
front of it, a noble building.

The inhabitants of these cities are proud
of them, and envious of each other with a
bitter rivalry. They do not love their cities
as a Manchester man loves Manchester or a

Münchener Munich, for they have probably lately arrived in them, and will surely pass on soon. But while they are there they love them, and with no silent love. They boost. To boost is to commend outrageously. And each cries up his own city, both from pride, it would appear, and for profit. For the fortunes of Newville are very really the fortunes of its inhabitants. From the successful speculator, owner of whole blocks, to the waiter bringing you a Martini, who has paid up a fraction of the cost of a quarter-share in a town-lot— all are the richer, as well as the prouder, if Newville grows. It is imperative to praise Edmonton in Edmonton. But it is sudden death to praise it in Calgary. The partisans of each city proclaim its superiority to all the others in swiftness of growth, future population, size of buildings, price of land— by all recognised standards of excellence. I travelled from Edmonton to Calgary in the company of a citizen of Edmonton and a citizen of Calgary. Hour after hour they disputed. Land in Calgary had risen from five dollars to three hundred; but in Edmonton from three to five hundred. Edmonton had grown from thirty persons to forty thousand in twenty years; but Calgary

from twenty to thirty thousand in twelve. . . .
" Where "—as a respite—" did I come from ? "
I had to tell them, not without shame, that
my own town of Grantchester, having num-
bered three hundred at the time of Julius
Cæsar's landing, had risen rapidly to nearly
four by Doomsday Book, but was now declined
to three-fifty. They seemed perplexed and
angry.

Sentimental people in the East will talk of
the romance of the West, and of these simple,
brave pioneers who have wrung a living from
the soil, and are properly proud of the rude
little towns that mark their conquest over
nature. That may apply to the frontiers of
civilisation up North, but the prairie-towns
have progressed beyond all that. A few of
the old pioneers of the West survive to watch
with startled eyes the wonderful fruits of
the seed they sowed. Such are among the
finest people in Canada, very different from
the younger generation, with wider interests,
good talkers, the best of company. From
them, and from records, one can learn of the
early settlers and the beginnings of the North-
West Mounted Police. The Police seem to
have been superb. For no great reward, but
the love of the thing, they imposed order and

fairness upon half a continent. The Indians trusted them utterly ; they were without fear. A store stands now in Calgary where forty years ago a policeman was shot to death by a murderer, followed over a thousand miles. He knew that the criminal would shoot ; but it was the rule of the Mounted Police not to fire first. Wounded, he killed his man, then died. And there was the case of the desperado who crossed the border, and was eventually captured and held by an immense force of American police and military. They awaited a regiment of the Police to conduct the villain back to trial. Two appeared, and being asked, " Where is the escort ? " replied, " We are the escort," and started back their five hundred miles ride with the murderer in tow. And there were the two who pursued a horse-thief from Dawson down to Minneapolis, caught him, and took him back to Dawson to be hanged. And there was the settler, who . . .

The tragedy of the West is that these men have passed, and that what they lived and died to secure for their race is now the foundation for a gigantic national gambling of a most unprofitable and disastrous kind. Hordes of people—who mostly seem to come from the great neighbouring Commonwealth, and are inspired with the national hunger for getting rich quickly without deserving it—prey on the community by their dealings in what is humorously called ' Real Estate.' For them our fathers died. What a sowing, and what a harvest ! And where good men worked or perished is now a row of little shops, all devoted to the sale of town-lots in some distant spot that must infallibly become a great city in the next two years, and in the doorway of each lounges a thin-chested, much-spitting youth, with a flabby face, shifty eyes, and an inhuman mouth, who invites you continually, with the most raucous of American accents, to " step inside and ex-amine our Praposition."

XII

THE INDIANS

XII

THE INDIANS

WHEN I was in the East, I got to know a man who had spent many years of his life living among the Indians. He showed me his photographs. He explained one, of an old woman. He said, " They told me there was an old woman in the camp called Laughing Earth. When I heard the name, I just said, ' Take me to her ! ' She wouldn't be photographed. She kept turning her back to me. I just picked up a clod and plugged it at her, and said, ' Turn round, Laughing Earth ! ' She turned half round, and grinned. She *was* a game old bird ! I joshed all the boys here Laughing Earth was my girl—till they saw her photo ! "

There stands Laughing Earth, in brightly-coloured petticoat and blouse, her grey hair blowing about her. Her back is towards you, but her face is turned, and scarcely hidden by a hand that is raised with all the coyness of seventy years. Laughter shines from the infinitely lined, round, brown cheeks, and from the mouth, and from the dancing eyes, and floods and spills over from each of the innumerable wrinkles. Laughing Earth—there is endless vitality in that laughter. The hand and face and the old body laugh. No skinny, intellectual mirth, affecting but the lips ! It was the merriment of an apple bobbing on the bough, or a brown stream running over rocks, or any other gay creature of earth. And with all was a great dignity, invulnerable to clods, and a kindly and noble beauty. By the light of that laughter much becomes clear—the right place of man upon earth, the entire suitability in life of very brightly-coloured petticoats, and the fact that old age is only a different kind of a merriment from youth, and a wiser.

And by that light the fragments of this pathetic race become more comprehensible, and, perhaps, less pathetic. The wanderer in Canada sees them from time to time, the more the further west he goes, irrelevant and inscrutable figures. In the east, French and Scotch half-breeds frequent the borders of ciyilisation. In any western town you may chance on a brave and his wife and a baby, resplendent in gay blankets and trappings, sliding gravely through the hideousness of the new order that has supplanted them. And there will be a few half-breeds loitering at the corners of the streets. These people of mixed race generally seem unfortunate in the first generation. A few of the older ones, the 'old-timers,' have 'made good,' and hold positions in the society for which they pioneered. But most appear to inherit the weaknesses of both sides. Drink does its work. And the nobler ones, like the tragic figure of that poetess who died recently, Pauline Johnson, seem fated to be at odds with the world. The happiest, whether Indian or half-breed, are those who live beyond the ever-advancing edges of cultivation and order, and force a livelihood from nature by hunting and fishing. Go anywhere into the wild, and you will find in little clearings, by lake or river, a dilapidated hut with a family of these solitaries, friendly with the pioneers or trappers around, ready to act as guide on hunt or trail. The Government, extraordinarily painstaking and well-intentioned, has established Indian schools, and trains some of them to take their places in the civilisation we have built. Not the best Indians these, say lovers of the race. I have met them, as clerks or stenographers, only distinguishable from their neighbours by a darker skin and a sweeter voice and manner. And in a generation or two, I suppose, the strain mingles and is lost. So we finish with kindness what our fathers began with war.

The Government, and others, have scientifically studied the history and characteristics of the Indians, and written them down in books, lest it be forgotten that human beings could be so extraordinary. They were a wandering race, it appears, of many tribes and, even, languages. Not apt to arts or crafts, they had, and have, an unrefined delight in bright colours. They enjoyed a ' Nature-Worship,' believed rather dimly in a presiding Power, and very definitely in certain ethical and moral rules. One of their incomprehensible customs was that at certain intervals the tribe divided itself into two factitious divisions, each headed by various chiefs, and gambled furiously for many days, one party against the other. They were pugnacious, and in their uncivilised way fought frequent wars. They were remarkably loyal to each other, and treacherous to the foe ; brave, and very stoical. " Monogamy was very prevalent." It is remarked that husbands and wives were very fond of each other, and the great body of scientific opinion favours the theory that mothers were much attached to their children. Most tribes were very healthy, and some fine-looking. Such were the remarkable people who hunted, fought, feasted, and·lived here until the light came, and all was changed. Other qualities they had even more remarkable to a European, such as utter honesty, and complete devotion to the truth among themselves. Civilisation, disease, alcohol, and vice have reduced them to a few scattered communities and some stragglers, and a legend, the admiration of boyhood. Boys they were, pugnacious, hunters, loyal, and cruel, older than the merrier children of the South Seas, younger and simpler than the weedy, furtive, acquisitive youth who may figure our age and type. " We must be a Morally Higher race than the Indians," said an earnest American businessman to me in Saskatoon, " because we have Survived them. The Great Darwin has proved it." I visited, later, a community of our Moral Inferiors, an Indian ' reservation ' under the shade of the Rockies. The Government has put aside various tracts of land where the Indians may conduct their lives in something of their old way, and stationed in each an agent to protect their interests. For every white man, as an agent told me, " thinks an Indian legitimate prey for all forms of cheating and robbery."

The reservations are the better in proportion as they are further from the towns and cities. The one I saw was peopled by a few hundred Stonies, one of the finest and most untouched of the tribes. Of these Laughing Earth had made one, but alas! a few years before she had become

> "a portion of the mirthfulness
> That once she made more mirthful."

The Indians occupy themselves with a little farming and hunting, and with expeditions, and live in two or three small scattered villages of huts and tents. But the centre of the community is the little white-washed house where the agent has his office. Here we sat, he and I, and talked, behind the counter. The agent is father, mother, clergyman, tutor, physician, solicitor, and banker to the Indians. They wandered in and out of the place with their various requests. The most part of them could not talk English, but there was generally some young Indian to interpret. An old chief entered. His grey hair curled down to his broad shoulders. He had, a noble forehead, brown, steady eyes, a thin, humorous mouth. His cow had been run over by the C.P.R. What was to be done? and how much would he get? The affair was discussed through an interpreter, a Canadianised young Indian in trousers, who spat. Some of the men, especially the older ones, have wonderful dignity and beauty of face and body. Their physique is superb; their features shaped and lined by weather and experience into a Roman nobility that demands respect. Several such passed through. Then came an old woman, wizened and loquacious, bent double by the sack of her weekly provision of meat and flour. She required oil, was given it, secreted it in some cranny of the many-coloured bundle that she was, and staggered creakily off again.

The office emptied for a while. Then drifted in a younger man, tall, with that brown, dog-like expression of simplicity many Indians wear. He was covered by a large grey-coloured blanket, over his other clothes. He puffed at a pipe and stared out of the window. The agent and I continued talking.

You must never hurry an Indian. Presently he gave a little grunt. The agent said, "Well, John?" John went on smoking. Five minutes later, in the middle of our conversation, John said suddenly, "Salt." He was staring inexpressively at the ceiling. "Why, John," said the agent, "I gave you enough salts on Thursday to last you a week." John directed his gaze on us, and smoked dumbly. "Still the stomach?" inquired the agent, genially. John's expression became gradually grimmer, and he moved one hand slowly across till it rested on his stomach. An impassive, significant hand. After a courteous pause the agent rose, poured some Epsom salts out of a large jar, wrapped them in paper, and handed them over. John secreted them dispassionately in some pouch among the skins and blankets that wrapped him in. We went back to our conversation. Five minutes after he grunted, suddenly. Again five minutes, and he departed. His wife—a plump, patient young woman—and his solemn-eyed, fat, ridiculous son of four, were sitting stolidly on the grass outside. It obviously made no difference if he took one hour or seven over his business. They mounted their tiny ponies and trotted briskly off. . . .

I suppose one is apt to be sentimental about these good people. They're really so picturesque; they trail clouds of Fenimore Cooper; and they seem, for all their unfitness, reposefully more in touch with permanent things than the America that has succeeded them. And it is interesting to watch our pathetic efforts to prevent or disarm the effects of ourselves. What will happen? Shall we preserve these few bands of them, untouched, to succeed us, ultimately, when the grasp of our ' civilisation ' weakens, and our transient anarchy in these wilder lands recedes once more before the older anarchy of Nature ? Or will they be entirely swallowed by that ugliness of shops and trousers with which we enchain the earth, and become a memory and less than a memory ? They are that already. The Indians have passed. They left no arts, no tradition, no buildings or roads or laws; only a story or two, and a few names, strange and beautiful. The ghosts of the old chiefs must surely chuckle when they note that the name by which Canada has called her capital and the centre of her political life, Ottawa, is an Indian name which signifies ' buying and selling.' And the wanderer in this land will always be remarking an unexplained fragrance about the place-names, as from some flower which has withered, and which he does not know.

XIII

THE ROCKIES

XIII

THE ROCKIES

At Calgary, if you can spare a minute from more important matters, slip beyond the hurrying white city, climb the golf links, and gaze west. A low bank of dark clouds disturbs you by the fixity of its outline. It is the Rockies, seventy miles away. On a good day, it is said, they are visible twice as far, so clear and serene is this air. Five hundred miles west is the coast of British Columbia, a region with a different climate, different country, and different problems. It is cut off from the prairies by vast tracts of wild country and uninhabitable ranges. For nearly two hundred miles the train pants through the homeless grandeur of the Rockies and the Selkirks. Four or five hotels, a few huts or tents, and a rare mining-camp—that is all the habitation in many thousands of square miles. Little even of that is visible from the train. That is one of the chief differences between the effect of the Rockies and

that of the Alps. There, you are always in
sight of a civilisation which has nestled for
ages at the feet of those high places. They
stand, enrobed with worship, and grander by
contrast with the lives of men. These un-
memoried heights are inhuman—or rather,
irrelevant to humanity. No recorded Hannibal
has struggled across them ; their shadow lies
on no remembered literature. They acknow-
ledge claims neither of the soul nor of the
body of man. He is a stranger, neither
Nature's enemy nor her child. She is there
alone, scarcely a unity in the heaped confusion
of these crags, almost without grandeur among
the chaos of earth.

Yet this horrid and solitary wildness is but
one aspect. There is beauty here, at length,
for the first time in Canada, the real beauty
that is always too sudden for mortal eyes, and
brings pain with its comfort. The Rockies
have a remoter, yet a kindlier, beauty than
the Alps. Their rock is of a browner colour,
and such rugged peaks and crowns as do
not attain snow continually suggest gigantic
castellations, or the ramparts of Titans. East-
ward, the foothills are few and low, and the
mountains stand superbly. The heart lifts
to see them. They guard the sunset. Into

this rocky wilderness you plunge, and toil through it hour by hour, viewing it from the rear of the Observation-Car. The Observation-Car is a great invention of the new world. At the end of the train is a compartment with large windows, and a little platform behind it, roofed over, but exposed otherwise to the air. On this platform are sixteen little perches, for which you fight with Americans. Victorious, you crouch on one, and watch the ever-receding panorama behind the train. It is an admirable way of viewing scenery. But a day of being perpetually drawn backwards at a great pace through some of the grandest mountains in the world has a queer effect. Like life, it leaves you with a dizzy irritation. For, as in life, you never see the glories till they are past, and then they vanish with incredible rapidity. And if you crane to see the dwindling further peaks, you miss the new splendours.

The day I went through most of the Rockies was, by some standards, a bad one for the view. Rain scudded by in forlorn, grey showers, and the upper parts of the mountains were wrapped in cloud, which was but rarely blown aside to reveal the heights. Sublimity, therefore, was left to the imagination ; but desolation was most vividly present. In no weather could the impression of loneliness be stronger. The pines drooped and sobbed. Cascades, born somewhere in the dun firmament above, dropped down the mountain sides in ever-growing white threads. The rivers roared and plunged with aimless passion down the ravines. Stray little clouds, left behind when the wrack lifted a little, ran bleating up and down the forlorn hill-sides. More often, the clouds trailed along the valleys, a long procession of shrouded, melancholy figures, seeming to pause, as with an indeterminate, tragic, vain gesture, before passing out of sight up some ravine.

Yet desolation is not the final impression that will remain of the Rockies and the Selkirks. I was advised by various people to ' stop off ' at Banff and at Lake Louise, in the Rockies. I did so. They are supposed to be equally the beauty-spots of the mountains. How perplexing it is that advisers are always so kindly and willing to help, and always so undiscriminating. It is equally disastrous to be a sceptic and to be credulous. Banff is an ordinary little tourist-resort in mountainous country, with hills and a stream and snow-peaks beyond. Beautiful enough, and in-

vigorating. But Lake Louise—Lake Louise
is of another world. Imagine a little round
lake 6000 feet up, a mile across, closed in by
great cliffs of brown rock, round the shoulders
of which are thrown mantles of close dark
pine. At one end the lake is fed by a vast
glacier, and its milky tumbling stream ; and
the glacier climbs to snowfields of one of the
highest and loveliest peaks in the Rockies,
which keeps perpetual guard over the scene.
To this place you go up three or four miles
from the railway. There is the hotel at one
end of the lake, facing the glacier ; else no
sign of humanity. From the windows you
may watch the water and the peaks all day,
and never see the same view twice. In the
lake, ever-changing, is Beauty herself, as
nearly visible to mortal eyes as she may ever
be. The water, beyond the flowers, is green,
always a different green. Sometimes it is
tranquil, glassy, shot with blue, of a peacock
tint. Then a little wind awakes in the distance, and ruffles the surface, yard by yard,
covering it with a myriad tiny wrinkles, till
half the lake is milky emerald, while the rest
still sleeps. And, at length, the whole is
astir, and the sun catches it, and Lake Louise
is a web of laughter, the opal distillation of all

the buds of all the spring. On either side
go up the dark processional pines, mounting
to the sacred peaks, devout, kneeling, motion-
less, in an ecstasy of homely adoration, like
the donors and their families in a Flemish
picture. Among these you may wander for
hours by little rambling paths, over white
and red and golden flowers, and, continually,
you spy little lakes, hidden away, each a shy,
soft jewel of a new strange tint of green or
blue, mutable and lovely. . . . And beyond
all is the glacier and the vast fields and peaks
of eternal snow.

If you watch the great white cliff, from the
foot of which the glacier flows—seven miles
away, but it seems two—you will sometimes
see a little puff of silvery smoke go up, thin,
and vanish. A few seconds later comes the
roar of terrific, distant thunder. The mountains tower and smile unregarding in the sun.
It was an avalanche. And if you climb any
of the ridges or peaks around, there are discovered other valleys and heights and ranges,
wild and desert, stretching endlessly away.
As day draws to an end the shadows on the
snow turn bluer, the crying of innumerable
waters hushes, and the immense, bare ramparts
of westward-facing rock that guard the great

valley win a rich, golden-brown radiance. Long after the sun has set they seem to give forth the splendour of the day, and the tranquillity of their centuries, in undiminished fulness. They have that other-worldly serenity which a perfect old age possesses. And as with a perfect old age, so here, the colour and the light ebb so gradually out of things that you could swear nothing of the radiance and glory gone up to the very moment before the dark.

It was on such a height, and at some such hour as this, that I sat and considered the nature of the country in this continent. There was perceptible, even here, though less urgent than elsewhere, the strangeness I had noticed in woods by the St Lawrence, and on the banks of the Delaware (where are red-haired girls who sing at dawn), and in British Columbia, and afterwards among the brown hills and colossal trees of California, but especially by that lonely golden beach in Manitoba, where the high-stepping little brown deer run down to drink, and the wild geese through the evening go flying and crying. It is an empty land. To love the country here—mountains are worshipped, not loved—is like embracing a wraith. A European can find nothing to satisfy the hunger of his heart. The air is too thin to breathe. He requires haunted woods, and the friendly presence of ghosts The immaterial soil of England is heavy and fertile with the decaying stuff of past seasons and generations. Here is the floor of a new wood, yet uncumbered by one year's autumn fall. We Europeans find the Orient stale and too luxuriantly fetid by reason of the multitude of bygone lives and thoughts, oppressive with the crowded presence of the dead, both men and gods. So, I imagine, a Canadian would feel our woods and fields heavy with the past and the invisible, and suffer claustrophobia in an English countryside beneath the dreadful pressure of immortals. For his own forests and wild places are windswept and empty. That is their charm, and their terror. You may lie awake all night and never feel the passing of evil presences, nor hear printless feet ; neither do you lapse into slumber with the comfortable consciousness of those friendly watchers who sit invisibly by a lonely sleeper under an English sky. Even an Irishman would not see a row of little men with green caps lepping along beneath the fire-weed and the golden daisies ; nor have the subtler fairies of England found

these wilds. It has never paid a steamship
or railway company to arrange for their
emigration.

In the bush of certain islands of the South
Seas you may hear a crashing on windless
noons, and, looking up, see a corpse swinging
along head downwards at a great speed from
tree to tree, holding by its toes, grimacing,
dripping with decay. Americans, so active
in this life, rest quiet afterwards. And
though every stone of Wall Street have its
separate Lar, their kind have not gone out
beyond city-lots. The maple and the birch
conceal no dryads, and Pan has never been
heard amongst these reed-beds. Look as long
as you like upon a cataract of the New World,
you shall not see a white arm in the foam. A
godless place. And the dead do not return.
That is why there is nothing lurking in the
heart of the shadows, and no human mystery
in the colours, and neither the same joy nor the
kind of peace in dawn and sunset that older
lands know. It is, indeed, a new world.
How far away seem those grassy, moonlit
places in England that have been Roman
camps or roads, where there is always serenity,
and the spirit of a purpose at rest, and the
sunlight flashes upon more than flint ! Here

one is perpetually a first-comer.   The land is virginal, the wind cleaner than elsewhere, and every lake new-born, and each day is the first day.   The flowers are less conscious than English flowers, the breezes have nothing to remember, and everything to promise.   There walk, as yet, no ghosts of lovers in Canadian lanes.   This is the essence of the grey freshness and brisk melancholy of this land.   And for all the charm of those qualities, it is also the secret of a European's discontent.   For it is possible, at a pinch, to do without gods. But one misses the dead.

XIV

SOME NIGGERS

XIV

SOME NIGGERS

" Look at those niggers! Whose are they?" (*An American Suffragist lady on board s.s. 'Ventura,' entering Pago-Pago Harbour, Samoa, October 1913. Apropos of the Samoans.*)

I suppose that if news came that the National Gallery was burnt down, one might feel, while hearing of the general damage, the rooms gutted or untouched, the Rembrandts and Titians saved, harmed, or lost, a sudden disproportionately keen little stab of wonder: " The Pisanello *St Hubert*," or " The Patinir *Flight into Egypt* — What's happened to *that*? " So now there must be a handful of wanderers here and there who, among all the major conflagration and disasters of nations and continents, have felt the tug of the question, " What of Samoa ? "

The South Sea Islands have an invincible glamour. Any bar in 'Frisco or Sydney will give you tales of seamen who slipped ashore in Samoa or Tahiti or the Marquesas for a month's holiday, five, ten, or twenty years ago.

Their wives and families await them yet. They are compound, these islands, of all legendary heavens. They are Calypso's and Prospero's isle, and the Hesperides, and Paradise, and every timeless and untroubled spot. Such tales have been made of them by men who have been there, and gone away, and have been haunted by the smell of the bush and the lagoons, and faint thunder on the distant reef, and the colours of sky and sea and coral, and the beauty and grace of the islanders. And the queer thing is that it's all, almost tiresomely, true. In the South Seas the Creator seems to have laid Himself out to show what He *can* do. Imagine an island with the most perfect climate in the world, tropical, yet almost always cooled by a breeze from the sea. No malaria or other fevers. No dangerous beasts, snakes, or insects. Fish for the catching, and fruits for the plucking. And an earth and sky and sea of immortal loveliness. What more could civilisation give ? Umbrellas ? Rope ? Gladstone bags ? . . . Any one of the vast leaves of the banana is more waterproof than the most expensive woven stuff. And from the first tree you can tear off a long strip of fibre that holds better than any rope. And thirty

seconds' work on a great palm-leaf produces
a basket-bag which will carry incredible
weights all day, and can be thrown away in
the evening. A world of conveniences. And
the things which civilisation has left behind
or missed by the way are there, too, among
the Polynesians: beauty and courtesy and
mirth. I think there is no gift of mind or
body that the wise value which these people
lack. A man I met in some other islands,
who had travelled much all over the world,
said to me, " I have found no man, in or out
of Europe, with the good manners and dignity
of the Samoan, with the possible exception of
the Irish peasant." A people among whom
an Italian would be uncouth, and a high-caste
Hindu vulgar, and Karsavina would seem
clumsy, and Helen of Troy a frump.

The white population of Heaven, as one
would expect, is very small; but, as one
wouldn't expect, it is composed of Americans,
English, and Germans. About half Germans,
for it has been a German colony for some
fourteen years. But it is one of the few white
' possessions,' I suppose, where a decent white
needn't feel ashamed of himself. For, though
it's proper to deny that Germans can colonise,
they have certainly ruled Samoa very well.

In some part, no doubt, the luck has been with them—with the world—in this success. Samoa was one of their later and wiser attempts in colonising. The first governor was Herr Solf, the present Secretary for the Colonies, who is reputed to have started the administration of Samoa after a careful examination of our method of ruling Fiji, and with a due, but not complete, regard for the advice of the chief English and American settlers in Samoa. Certainly he started it very ably and wisely. By luck and good management those various forces which might destroy the beauty of Samoa are almost ineffectual. The fact that the missionaries are nearly all English puts a slight sufficient chasm between the spiritual and civil powers, and avoids that worst peril of these places—hierocracy. The trade of the islands is largely a monopoly of the ' German firm,' a big affair which pays a few people in Hamburg fabulous percentages. So smaller traders aren't encouraged to flourish unduly ; and the German firm itself is too well fed to bother about extending. The Samoans, therefore, aren't exploited, spiritually or commercially, as much as they might be. By such slight chances beauty keeps a foothold in the world. The missionary's peace of mind may require that the Samoan should wear trousers, or the trader's pocket that he should drink gin and live under corrugated iron. But the Government has discovered that these things are not good for the health of the Polynesian, so the Samoan wears his *lava-lava* and drinks his *kava*, and lives in his cool and lovely thatched hut, and is happy. And—final test of administration—the population is no longer decreasing.

But I think there's more than luck or German wisdom at the bottom of the happy condition of Samoa. Something in the very magic of the place seems to subdue or soften the evil in men. Heaven forbid I should deny that mean and treacherous and cruel acts of white men and brown are on record. But as a rule the greedy or the boorish, once they settle there, appear to mellow and grow quiet. Between this sea and sky even a trader becomes almost a gentleman, even a Prussian almost lovable, and the very missionaries are betrayed by beauty, and contentment takes them unaware.

Samoa has been well governed. The people have been forbidden a few perils of civilisation, and for the rest are left pretty well to themselves. Go up from Apia across the mountains, or round the coast, or take a boat over to the other big island, Savaii, and you find them living their old life, fishing and bathing and singing, and never a sign of a white man. They are guaranteed possession of their land. They'll sometimes complain faintly of ' taxation '—a small head-tax the Government exacts, which compels the individual to some four or five days' work a year. The English inhabitants themselves have had no grumble against the Germans except that they incline to be ' too kind to the natives '—an admirable testimonial. And traders in the Pacific say they always get far better treatment from the customs and harbour authorities at Apia than at the British Suva, in Fiji.

And yet the Samoans do not like the Germans. When I was there, nearly a year ago, I was often asked, " When will Peritania (Britain) fight Germany, and send her away from Samoa ? " They have no complaint against the Germans. They have merely a sentimental and highly flattering preference for the English. On a recent visit of an English gunboat to Apia, the officers were entertained at a Samoan dinner party, with music and dances, by an eminent and very charming young princess. The princess is a famous beauty, with the keen intelligence Samoans have if they care, a wonderful dancer, possessed of a glorious singing voice and a perfect knowledge of English. The party was a great success. The princess led her guests afterwards to the flag-staff. Before anyone could stop her, she leapt on to the pole and raced up the sixty feet of it. That also is among the accomplishments of a Samoan princess. She seized the German flag, tore it to pieces, brought it down, and danced on it. So the tale is ; and it is probably true. In the villages where I stayed it was amusing how swiftly and completely the children forgot the few words of German the Government sometimes had them taught; while one or two common phrases, ' *Morgen,*' ' *gut,*' etc., were retained as extremely good jokes by the boys and girls, occasions of inextinguishable laughter, through the absurdity of their sound and the very ridiculous Germanness of them. . . .

I wish I were there again. It is a country, and a life, that bind the heart. There is a poem :

> " I know an island,
>   Lovely and lost, and half the world away ;
>   And there, 'twixt lowland and highland,

Lies a pool, rich with murmur and scent and glimmer,
And there my friends go, all the radiant day,
Each golden-limbed and flower-crowned laughing swimmer,"

—and so on. It tells how ugly and joyless by comparison the fellow's own country sometimes seems, filled with money-making and fogs and such grey things :

"Evil, and gloom, and cold o' nights in my land;
   But,—I know an island
   Where Beauty and Courtesy, as flowers, blow."

So it goes, with a jolly return on the rhyme. But the whole poem is a bad one. Still, the man felt it, the magic. It is a magic of a different way of life. In the South Seas, if you live the South Sea life, the intellect soon lapses into quiescence. The body becomes more active, the senses and perceptions more lordly and acute. It is a life of swimming and climbing and resting after exertion. The skin seems to grow more sensitive to light and air, and the feel of water and the earth and leaves. Hour after hour one may float in the warm lagoons, conscious, in the whole body, of every shred and current of the multitudinous water, or diving under in a vain attempt to catch the radiant butterfly-coloured fish that flit in and out of the thousand windows of their gorgeous coral palaces. Or go up, one of a singing flower-garlanded crowd, to a shaded pool of a river in the bush, cool from the mountains. The blossom-hung darkness is streaked with the bodies that fling themselves, head or feet first, from the cliffs around the water, and the haunted forest-silence is broken by laughter. It is part of the charm of these people that, while they are not so foolish as to 'think,' their intelligence is incredibly lively and subtle, their sense of humour and their intuitions of other people's feelings are very keen and living. They have built up, in the long centuries of their civilisation, a delicate and noble complexity of behaviour and of personal relationships. A white man living with them soon feels his mind as deplorably dull as his skin is pale and unhealthy among those glorious golden-brown bodies. But even he soon learns to *be* his body (and so his true mind), instead of using it as a stupid convenience for his personality, a moment's umbrella against this world. He is perpetually and intensely aware of the subtleties of taste in food, of every tint and line of the incomparable glories of those dawns and evenings, of each shade of intercourse in fishing or swimming or dancing with the best companions in the world. That alone is life; all else is death. And after dark, the black palms against a tropic night, the smell of the wind, the tangible moonlight like a white, dry, translucent mist, the lights in the huts, the murmur and laughter of passing figures, the passionate, queer thrill of the rhythm of some hidden dance—all this will seem to him, inexplicably and almost unbearably, a scene his heart has known long ago, and forgotten, and yet always looked for.

And now Samoa is ours. A New Zealand Expeditionary Force took it. Well, I know a princess who will have had the day of her life. Did they see Stevenson's tomb gleaming high up on the hill, as they made for that passage in the reef? Did Vasa, with his heavy-lidded eyes, and that infinitely adorable lady Fafaia, wander down to the beach to watch them land? They must have landed from boats; and at noon, I see. How hot they got! I know that Apia noon. Didn't they rush to the Tivoli bar—but I forget, New Zealanders are teetotalers. So, perhaps, the Samoans gave them the coolest of all drinks, *kava*; and they scored. And what dances in their honour, that night !—but, again, I'm afraid the *houla-houla* would shock

a New Zealander. I suppose they left a
garrison, and went away. I can very vividly
see them steaming out in the evening; and
the crowd on shore would be singing them that
sweetest and best-known of South Sea songs,
which begins ' Good-bye, my Flenni ' (' Friend,'
you'd pronounce it), and goes on in Samoan,
a very beautiful tongue. I hope they'll rule
Samoa well.

AN UNUSUAL YOUNG MAN

AN UNUSUAL YOUNG MAN

SOME say the Declaration of War threw us into a primitive abyss of hatred and the lust for blood. Others declare that we behaved very well. I do not know. I only know the thoughts that flowed through the mind of a friend of mine when he heard the news. My friend—I shall make no endeavour to excuse him—is a normal, even ordinary man, wholly English, twenty-four years old, active and given to music. By a chance he was ignorant of the events of the world during the last days of July. He was camping with some friends in a remote part of Cornwall, and had gone on, with a companion, for a four-days' sail. So it wasn't till they beached her again that they heard. A youth ran down to them with a telegram : " We're at war with Germany. We've joined France and Russia."

My friend ate and drank, and then climbed a hill of gorse, and sat alone, looking at the sea. His mind was full of confused images, and the sense of strain. In answer to the word 'Germany,' a train of vague thoughts dragged across his brain. The pompous middle-class vulgarity of the building of Berlin; the wide and restful beauty of Munich; the taste of beer; innumerable quiet, glittering *cafés*; the *Ring*; the swish of evening air in the face, as one *skis* down past the pines; a certain angle of the eyes in the face; long nights of drinking, and singing and laughter; the admirable beauty of German wives and mothers; certain friends; some tunes; the quiet length of evening over the Starnberger-See. Between him and the Cornish sea he saw quite clearly an April morning on a lake south of Berlin, the grey water slipping past his little boat, and a peasant-woman, suddenly revealed against apple-blossom, hanging up blue and scarlet garments to dry in the sun. Children played about her; and she sang as she worked. And he remembered a night in Munich spent with a students' *Kneipe*. From eight to one they had continually emptied immense jugs of beer, and smoked, and sung English and German songs in profound chorus. And when the party broke up he found himself arm-in-arm with the president, who was a vast Jew, and with an Apollonian youth called Leo Diringer, who said he was a poet. There was also a fourth

man, of whom he could remember no detail.
Together, walking with ferocious care down
the middle of the street, they had swayed
through Schwabing seeking an open *café*.
Café Benz was closed, but further up there
was a little place still lighted, inhabited by
one waiter, innumerable chairs and tables
piled on each other for the night, and a row
of chess-boards, in front of which sat a little
bald, bearded man in dress-clothes, waiting.
The little man seemed to them infinitely
pathetic. Four against one, they played him
at chess, and were beaten. They bowed,
and passed into the night. Leo Diringer
recited a sonnet, and slept suddenly at the
foot of a lamp-post. The Jew's heavy-lidded
eyes shone with a final flicker of caution, and
he turned homeward resolutely, to the last
not wholly drunk. My friend had wandered
to his lodgings, in an infinite peace. He could
not remember what had happened to the
fourth man. . . .

A thousand little figures tumbled through
his mind. But they no longer brought with
them that air of comfortable kindliness which
Germany had always signified for him. Something in him kept urging, " You must hate
these things, find evil in them." There was

that half-conscious agony of breaking a mental habit, painting out a mass of associations, which he had felt in ceasing to believe in a religion, or, more acutely, after quarrelling with a friend. He knew that was absurd. The picture came to him of encountering the Jew, or Diringer, or old Wolf, or little Streckmann, the pianist, in a raid on the East Coast, or on the Continent, slashing at them in a stagey, dimly-imagined battle. Ridiculous. He vaguely imagined a series of heroic feats, vast enterprise, and the applause of crowds. . . .

From that egotism he was awakened to a different one, by the thought that this day meant war and the change of all things he knew. He realised, with increasing resentment, that music would be neglected. And he wouldn't be able, for example, to camp out. He might have to volunteer for military training and service. Some of his friends would be killed. The Russian ballet wouldn't return. His own relationship with A——, a girl he intermittently adored, would be changed. Absurd, but inevitable ; because —he scarcely worded it to himself—he and she and everyone else were going to be different. His mind fluttered irascibly to escape from this thought, but still came back to it, like a tethered bird. Then he became calmer, and wandered out for a time into fantasy.

A cloud over the sun woke him to consciousness of his own thoughts; and he found, with perplexity, that they were continually recurring to two periods of his life, the days after the death of his mother, and the time of his first deep estrangement from one he loved. After a bit he understood this. Now, as then, his mind had been completely divided into two parts: the upper running about aimlessly from one half-relevant thought to another, the lower unconscious half labouring with some profound and unknowable change. This feeling of ignorant helplessness linked him with those past crises. His consciousness was like the light scurry of waves at full tide, when the deeper waters are pausing and gathering and turning home. Something was growing in his heart, and he couldn't tell what. But as he thought 'England and Germany,' the word 'England' seemed to flash like a line of foam. With a sudden tightening of his heart, he realised that there might be a raid on the English coast. He didn't imagine any possibility of it *succeeding*, but only of enemies and warfare on English soil. The idea sickened him. He was im-

mensely surprised to perceive that the actual
earth of England held for him a quality which
he found in A——, and in a friend's honour,
and scarcely anywhere else, a quality which,
if he'd ever been sentimental enough to use
the word, he'd have called ' holiness.' His
astonishment grew as the full flood of
' England ' swept him on from thought to
thought. He felt the triumphant helplessness
of a lover. Grey, uneven little fields, and
small, ancient hedges rushed before him, wild
flowers, elms and beeches, gentleness, sedate
houses of red brick, proudly unassuming, a
countryside of rambling hills and friendly
copses. He seemed to be raised high, looking
down on a landscape compounded of the
western view from the Cotswolds, and the
Weald, and the high land in Wiltshire, and
the Midlands seen from the hills above Prince's
Risborough. And all this to the accompaniment of tunes heard long ago, an intolerable
number of them being hymns. There was,
in his mind, a confused multitude of faces,
to most of which he could not put a name.
At one moment he was on an Atlantic liner,
sick for home, making Plymouth at nightfall ;
and at another, diving into a little rocky pool
through which the Teign flows, north of Bovey ;

and again, waking, stiff with dew, to see the dawn come up over the Royston plain. And continually he seemed to see the set of a mouth which he knew for his mother's, and A——'s face, and, inexplicably, the face of an old man he had once passed in a Warwick-shire village. To his great disgust, the most commonplace sentiments found utterance in him. At the same time he was extraordinarily happy. . . .

My friend, who has always, though never very passionately, believed himself a most unusual young man, rose to his feet. Feeling a little frightened, and more than a little unwell—for he is a person of quiet mental habits—he wandered down the hill. He kept slowly moving his head, like a man who wishes to dodge a pain. I gather that he was conscious of few definite thoughts till he reached the London train. He kept remem-bering, unwillingly, a midnight in Carnival-time in Munich, when he had seen a clown, a Pierrot, and a Columbine tip-toe deli-cately round the deserted corner of Theresien-strasse, and vanish into the darkness. Then he thought of the lights on the pavement in Trafalgar Square. It seemed to him the most desirable thing in the world to mingle and talk with a great many English people. Also, he kept saying to himself—for he felt vaguely jealous of the young men in Germany and France—" Well, if Armageddon's *on*, I suppose one should be there." . . . Of France, he tells me, he thought little. The French always seemed to him people to be respected, but very remote ; more incomprehensible than the Japanese, more, even, than the Irish. Of Russia, less. She meant nothing to him except a sense of hysteria and vague evil which he had been given by some of her music and literature. He thought often and heavily of Germany. Of England, all the time. He didn't know whether he was glad or sad. It was a new feeling.